REGIONAL PLANNING

REGIONAL PLANNING
INTRODUCTION & EXPLANATION

MELVILLE C. BRANCH

1988

PRAEGER

New York
Westport, Connecticut
London

Book and page design and illustrations by the author
Set in 11-point Palatino typeface by Graphic Typesetting
  Service, Los Angeles, CA
Photo negatives by Westside Processing, Los Angeles, CA
Word Processing by Ms. Colleen Edwards

Library of Congress Cataloging-in-Publication Data

Branch, Melville Campbell, 1913-
  Regional planning: introduction and explanation / Melville C. Branch.
  p. cm.
  Includes index.
  ISBN 0-275-92403-3 (alk. paper)
  ISBN 0-275-92539-0 (pbk.: alk. paper)
  1. Regional planning—United States. I. Title.
HT392.B72   1988   87-27314
361.6'0973—dc19   CIP

Library of Congress Catalog Card Number: 87-27314
ISBN: 0-275-92403-3
ISBN: 0-275-92539-0 (pbk.)
First published in 1988

Praeger Publishers, One Madison Avenue, New York, NY 10010
A division of Greenwood Press, Inc.

Printed in the United States of America

The paper used in this book complies with the Permanent Paper Standard issued
by the National Information Standards Organization (Z39.48–1984).

10 9 8 7 6 5 4 3 2 1

ACKNOWLEDGMENTS

The individuals noted alphabetically below have assisted the author in his research or writing in so many different ways that space does not permit specific explanation. Their contributions are gratefully acknowledged.

Bill Abbott, Balfrey & Abbott, Sacramento, CA; Mohammad Hussain Awad, Ph.D. Candidate, School of Urban and Regional Planning, University of Southern California, Los Angeles, CA; Dean E. Borton, Director of Communications, Calavo Growers of California, Los Angeles, CA; Keith Chandler, Assistant Production Manager, Riverside Printing Facility, *The Wall Street Journal*, Dow Jones & Co., Riverside, CA; William Day, Business Editor, Praeger Special Studies-Praeger Scientific, New York, NY; Commander David L. Dillon USN, Director, Navy Office of Information, Los Angeles, CA; Colleen Edwards, Los Angeles Psychoanalytic Society and Institute, Los Angeles, CA; Petty Officer Charles Embleton, Public Affairs Office, 11th Coast Guard District, Long Beach, CA; Virgil F. Fairchild, Manager, Market Research, NAVISTAR International Corporation, Chicago, IL; Dr. Heinrich von Ganseforth, Zweckverband Grossraum, Hannover, West Germany; Robert Giannanglia, Public Affairs Officer, U.S. Internal Revenue Service, Los Angeles District, CA; John W. Heaton III, Manager, Planning, The Coca-Cola Company, Atlanta, GA; Joyce Herman, Environmental Planner, Environmental Affairs, Southern California Edison Company, Rosemead, CA; Shiraz R. Kaderali, Director of Special Projects, Planning & Research, Pacific Gas and Electric Company, San Francisco, CA; Susan Kranzler, Public Affairs Specialist, Los Angeles District, Corps of Engineers, U.S. Department of the Army, Los Angeles, CA; Lee E. Koppelman, Executive Director, Long Island Regional Planning Board, Hauppauge, L.I., NY; Larry L. Kruckenberg, Chief, Communications, Game and Fish Department, The State of Wyoming, Cheyenne, WY; Aaron Levine, President, Oahu Development

Conference, Honolulu, HI; Shawn Moore, Plan and Procedures Specialist, U.S. Federal Aviation Administration, Los Angeles TRACON; Daniel W. O'Connell, Policy Coordinator, Growth Management Coordination, Office of Planning & Budgeting, Office of the Governor, State of Florida, Tallahassee, FL; Fred O'Donnell, Chief, Advertising and Sales Promotion, U.S. Army Recruiting Battalion, Los Angeles, CA; Thomas C. Richards, Lieutenant General, USAF, Commander, Headquarters Air University, U.S. Department of the Army, Maxwell Air Force Base, AL; Scott Ridgeway, Lab Manager, Westside Processing, Santa Monica, CA; Thomas I. Rubel, Management Horizons, Dublin, OH; Tim Skrove, Media Relations, The Metropolitan Water District of Southern California, Los Angeles, CA; Dennis B. Underwood, Executive Director, Colorado River Board of California, Los Angeles, CA.

Special appreciation is expressed to my wife—Hilda S. Rollman-Branch, M.D.—for her contribution to all my books by reading the first draft of my manuscript for clarity, and reviewing subsequent drafts in whole or in part to improve their quality.

PREFACE

The concept of regional space has existed since earliest times. The first humans were well aware of the living space required for their survival in a hostile environment. Through subsequent centuries various kinds of regions were identified in connection with civil governmental, military, business, academic, and other activities. Since the Industrial Revolution beginning in the early nineteenth century, great advances in scientific knowledge have added new regions relating to situations and conditions previously unknown or immeasurable.

The regional concept is employed in some way by most organizations and individuals. Different descriptive words may be used: area, district, territory, expanse, province, command, or theater of operations. But *region* is the common denominator term that applies to most of these different areas on the ground or in the air.

Research and reportive writing on the subject of regions have concentrated on identifying and analyzing particular areas displaying one or more common characteristics. Almost every field of study has identified such regions that reflect and add to its body of descriptive knowledge. Most of them are also employed in some practical analytical or operational way.

Among the best known regions are those used by the physical sciences: geography, geology, and meteorology. Economics, sociology, and politics also employ regional concepts in many of their evaluations of existing conditions and future prospects.

Another application has to do with socioeconomically depressed regions: how their local economies, social conditions, and physical facilities can be improved by national policies, regional planning, financial support, and investment directed to these ends. Much of the literature on regional planning has been produced on this application.

Studies have also been made relating to the establishment of special agencies to cope with particular problems extending across a number of local governmental jurisdictions. And proposals are advanced for the unified governance of metropolitan urban areas that encompass numerous legally independent municipalities within one continuously built-up urban expanse, so far with little success in the United States except for several forms of federally induced regional planning which yield limited results.

For two thousand years literature relating to cities and city planning has accumulated into an extensive body of reference materials. Except for descriptive geography, much less has been written about the various kinds and applications of regions. Although a variety of particular uses are familiar to those who employ them, there are few published works on the concept and utilization of regions by business organizations, private associations and institutions, and the military services. This may be due in part to competitive reticence or disclosure in the first two instances, and military security classification in the latter. It may also result from the greater emphasis by private enterprises and the military services on the application of regions in practice, rather than on research or reportive writing concerning them.

At present, there is no exposition of regions as a basic intellectual concept of wide applicability, great importance, and far-reaching consequences. Their fundamental nature, their function as factual descriptors of the real world, and their diverse operational use have not been treated in a single statement. Nor has the considerable knowledge concerning regions accumulated over the years in many places for different purposes been aggregated as a single subject.

Regions are important because of their descriptive significance and their employment in management and planning. As the world population passes five billion, as activities become technically more complex and environmentally more sensitive, regions are the areas of necessary attention and action since they define most accurately the spatially related conditions or problems.

With few exceptions these regions do not coincide with the jurisdictional boundaries of governmental units established for political purposes or as a consequence of historical events. This contradiction between the actual spatial situation or areal need and existing governmental jurisdictions poses a basic difficulty for planning.

Effective regional planning rather than jurisdictional planning is required to resolve or at least reduce the critical problems that increasingly beset the world, to improve the human condition, and to ensure human survival in the face of growing environmental threats. But the continuous cooperation between different governmental bodies necessary to effectuate regional planning is rarely achieved. Except in dire emergencies most individuals and institutions cooperate reluctantly and ineffectually.

As a consequence, comprehensive multiple-purpose regional planning in the United States is very rare.* Cooperation is largely limited to voluntary coordination of certain federally supported projects. However, since many problems that cannot be ignored involve large areas that include a number of independent governmental jurisdictions, regional agencies have been established each of which performs a single operational function within the district covered by its activities.

Environmental dangers are not yet so severe and threatening, nor the human condition so severely impaired, that the cooperation essential for comprehensive regional planning is considered essential rather than a matter of choice. But this

---

*In this book, reference is made to three different forms of planning: *comprehensive* (or system) planning by the highest directive authority, integrating all of the principal components of the organization or activity; *subsystem* planning by an intermediate level of directive management or control, correlating several closely interrelated elements of the organization or activity, but not all its principal components; and *functional* planning of one of the constituent components.

This set of definitions applies progressively to smaller organizational entities or more limited activities since they always consist of a number of component parts.

attitude is changing. The fact that regional planning is required for a habitable world and a hopeful human prospect is becoming increasingly apparent.

It is in anticipation of this development that this book is written. The concept of regions needs exposition and clarification in its broadest sense. The range and diversity of existing regions need to be comprehended, considered, and applied as needed. The critical importance of regional planning for the welfare and survival of the physical world and its animate inhabitants must be recognized. And the requirements and methods of accomplishing this most fundamental type of planning need to be identified.

For few fields is the Chinese proverb that a picture is worth a thousand words more appropriate than for regional planning. Regions are a spatial concept best portrayed in visual graphical form. They are difficult to describe by words alone. For some, verbal description would be extremely complicated and lengthy, impractical or impossible for general use. The utilization of regions in practice requires graphical expression.

For these reasons graphical illustrations are employed throughout this book. Because they are selected to best exemplify the many types and uses of regions, some are recent and others relate to situations or events years ago. They are simplified to the extent possible without loss of meaning. To facilitate their comparison, most regions are depicted on either of two base maps: one of the continental United States and the other an equal-area projection of the world. For the most part, written text is related to illustrations drawn by the author.

At the risk of oversimplification in a few instances, laymen's language is employed throughout this book. Technical terms and professional terminology are avoided because they prevent widespread understanding. The essence of most subjects can be expressed in the language appropriate for an introductory exposition.

Consideration of the full scope of the regional concept can be stimulating for those concerned with a particular application. They are alerted to the many forms and applications of this spatial designation. Recognition of the basic role of regions in human affairs may also encourage those disheartened by the limited comprehensive regional planning presently possible in the United States. Certainly, this book will introduce those interested but uninformed to the general subject of regions and regional planning.

The potential audience for this treatment of the subject is large. Most of the physical and social sciences, and most of the professions, are involved with regions. Most civil governmental agencies, the military services, businesses, private organizations and institutions are engaged in some form of regional analysis or activity.

More than one hundred colleges and universities in the United States offer introductory and advanced courses in "urban and regional planning." Some seventy schools award degrees in this field. Also involved with cities, regions, and their planning are public and business administration, civil engineering, law, architecture, and landscape architecture. Each of these related fields uses the regional concept for its own purposes or is concerned with regions as they are employed in planning.

This book can be used as a text or reference not only by the seven fields of education and professional practice noted in the previous paragraph, but by other fields concerned with regions in one way or another.

Identifying and analyzing different kinds and applications of regions as a single subject provides an initial formulation which can be extended some time in the future to constitute a more coherent and intellectually structured field of special knowledge. Such a formulation advances the quality of regional planning by civil government, business, and the military services. It promotes recognition that this form of planning is essential to the effective conduct of human activities, preservation of the physical environment, and improvement of the human prospect.

In its recognition of the region as a basic configuration in human life; in its acceptance of natural diversities as well as natural associations and uniformities; in its recognition of the region as a permanent sphere of cultural influences and as a center of economic activities, as well as an implicit geographic fact—here lies the vital common element in the regionalist movement. So, far from being archaic or reactionary, regionalism belongs to the future.

Mumford, Lewis, *The Culture of Cities*, New York, NY (Harcourt, Brace), 1938.

CONTENTS

ILLUSTRATIONS

The regional planning concept is itself remarkably elusive. In the scholarly texts and in popular usage, as well as in practical affairs, "region" is a flexible, almost generic, term, and there is general agreement that specific designations of regions must vary according to the needs, purposes, and standards involved in the designation.

Harvey Perloff, *Education for Planning: City, State, & Regional*, 1957.

PART I
TYPES, USES, PLANNING

In the United States, concern with regions and their delineation emerged somewhat later than in Europe. The country had to be explored and settled; climatic, soil, agricultural, social, economic, and other facts about it had to be recorded, compiled, and studied. Human groupings of people and interests had to emerge into consciousness and even rub against each other before there could develop in the United States a knowledge of regional realities, and a sense of the need for delimiting and utilizing regions for administrative and other purposes.

National Resources Committee, *Regional Factors in National Planning*, 1935.

CHAPTER 1
TYPES OF REGIONS

REGIONS ARE an inherent aspect of all animate life and behavior. The very existence of living organisms depends on physical conditions that permit their emergence, survival, and subsequent development. At the smallest scale, viruses, bacteria, and other microorganisms can exist only within certain microscopic spatial environments. Flora and fauna require particular climatological, geographical, geological, or other physical conditions to exist and flourish. In the beginning:

> As the earth's surface continued to cool, the clouds of steam filling the atmosphere could finally condense. Torrential rains fell for perhaps a hundred thousand years without cease, creating hot, shallow oceans. Submerged plate boundaries, rich in chemicals and energy, steadily vented hydrogen-rich gases into the seas. Water hitting the boiling lava in rifts and volcanoes evaporated, condensed and rained down again. . . . The waters rounded off the mountains as they were created, washing minerals and salts into the oceans and land pools. . . . Tectonic activity released gases in the earth's interior to form a new atmosphere. . . . The sun continued to beam heat and ultraviolet light into the earth's thickening atmosphere, as the fast-spinning planet spun in five-hour days and five-hour nights. The moon too had condensed from the sun's nebula. Our faithful natural satellite, rather large for a puny planet like the earth, from the beginning pulled rhythmically on the great bodies of water, creating tides.
>
> It is from this Archean Aeon, from 3,900 to 2,500 million years ago, that we have found the first traces of life. (Margulis, 1986)

Had these environments changed sufficiently over a short period of time, living organisms could not have evolved fast enough to adapt, nor could they migrate beyond the regional conditions essential for their continued existence. This interdependence between habitat and organism has characterized animate development on earth during several thousand million years and will maintain for the imaginable future.

Each organism has its own line of growth, that of its species, its own curve of development, its own span of variations, its own pattern of existence. To maintain its lifeshape the organism must constantly alter and renew itself by active relations with the rest of the environment. Even the most sessile and sleepy forms of life must seize energy in order to maintain their equilibrium: thus the organism changes, by no matter what infinitesimal amounts, this balance of the environment; and the failure to act and react means either the temporary suspension of life or its final end. Not merely is the organism implicated in its environment in space: it is also implicated in time, through the biological phenomena of inheritance and memory; and in human societies it is even more consciously implicated through the necessity of assimilating a complicated social heritage which forms, as it were, a second environment. (Mumford, 1938)

Most animals reflect their relationship to regions by their awareness of the kind and size of territory they need for their sustenance and reproduction. Many confirm this awareness by marking the territory they need to survive with scent or spoor, warning others of the same species to stay away. In much the same way, primitive people identified and marked as their own the territory they required to exist. Modern man does the same thing when he establishes political cartographic boundaries. People have always identified the best areas for hunting and fishing, farming, woodcutting, mining, and the many other human activities relating to the physical world that are important to survival, prosperity, or contentment.

Strong regional differences also existed [15,000 years ago]: the woolly mammoth and woolly rhinoceros were most numerous on the Russian plain and ibex lived in mountainous areas like the Pyrenees, as they do now. The many large herbivores were preyed upon by large populations of carnivores, including wolves and lions. (Museum of Natural History, 1986)

As knowledge advances and human activities become increasingly complex and technical, more regions are identified that are significant geographically, geologically, socioeconomically, administratively, politically, scientifically, or in some other way: for a civil governmental unit, military service, private enterprise, academic field, or other organization or individual—or for several or all of these together.

Despite this identification of numerous regions for many purposes, the regional concept is confusing for most people. We are accustomed to using the term as a general reference, identifying ourselves or someone else as from the South, North, Northeast, Northwest, or another part of the country. Such broad regional differentiation exists in music, literature, language, and other fields or areas of activity. We are aware of western and hillbilly music, the southern romantic novel, southern drawl and New England twang, or the eastern financial establishment.

[Ruth] Hale found that a rich and colorful variety of names were used to designate different regions. In total, 295 vernacular local regions were identified. The names used reflect the great variety of cultural, historical, and natural events and elements that have been noticed and experienced by the inhabitants. For example, in California, where regional consciousness was at a high level, seven separate subregions were commonly identified. Central Coast, Central Valley (San Joaquin), Sacramento Valley, and Sierra all are derived from physical features. Redwood Region shows an identification with the local vegetation, Mother Lode with a form of economic activity, and San Francisco Bay area with a political region. Other names, such as Little Dixie and Boonslick in Missouri, are historical in origin. (Saarinen, 1976)

Perhaps it is the large number and great diversity of regions, their widespread applicability and use, that create this confusion in the minds of many people. The term may seem so general and inclusive that it defies specific description, rigorous discussion, theoretical treatment, systematic formulation, or effective use.

But this is not the case in fact. *A region can be defined unambiguously as a sizeable space with one or more common characteristics established by nature or delineated by humans for descriptive, analytical, managerial, or other purposes.* So defined, regions can be employed in some way by almost every field of knowledge and applied to most human activities.

Words such as area, district, territory, theater, command, or special technical terms may be used instead of region. Normally, regions cover larger expanses than most areas and small districts. Some regions are small, but the term is seldom applied to very small areas and rarely to those that are microscopic. There is no upper limit to the size of a region; very large regions may be identified specifically by descriptive adjectives such as continental, global, or even galactic. The military services use the words command, theater, or a geographical term to designate large military regions.

areas   Strictly speaking, areas are two-dimensional spaces which can be described exactly by two linear measurements. Volume is space delineated by an area or surface and an additional third dimension.

While the areal dimensions of some regions are measured precisely, rarely is their spatial description completed by including the third dimension which exists for all regions in actuality. When this third dimension is very much smaller than the areal dimensions, as is most often the case, it is usually assumed rather than specified.

Unlike a region, an area can be defined and employed as a basic term without reference to its character or use. As a two-dimensional geometrical reference, it can be utilized at different times and places, for different purposes. For example, an acre or hectare, a square mile or a square kilometer are geometrical units of measurement with wide applicability. Areas can be very large or miniscule.

governmental   Governmental boundaries define a geographical realm,
boundaries   sovereignty, political or legal jurisdiction: historically established and politically fixed. Boundaries may change as a consequence of war or political action but this does not happen

often. Besides their obvious operational significance, governmental jurisdictions are informationally important because of the quantities of data descriptive of these jurisdictions collected over time by official censuses and surveys of all sorts, taken by a host of public and private organizations. Since the data relate to the same area, enumerations taken at different times for different purposes can be compared directly, without the statistical adjustment required when the area covered varies.

Regional boundaries rarely coincide with governmental jurisdictions unless they are adjusted to do so. They are determined by the natural characteristics of the physical world, or by human delineation for a single or multiple purposes. They are substantively rather than politically derived. They represent fundamental interrelationships between people or other living organisms and the spatial environment. As discussed in Chapter 3 on Regions and Planning, it is the basic difference between substantive regions and governmental jurisdictions that makes comprehensive regional planning so difficult to achieve.

When public utility and other special districts are established with limited governmental powers to provide a product such as water or electricity, or services such as public health care, air pollution or flood control, the geographical borders of each district are adjusted to the extent possible to coincide with the jurisdictions of general government. These governmental regions are, of course, supremely important because they are the areas within which the organized powers of society are exercised: political, legal, economic, social, and administrative. They are also the areas to which most official information is related.

Primitive people, whether nomadic or sedentary, could not *historical* exist and survive without access to a geographic region suffi- *examples* cient to provide water, food, and essential raw materials. In early recorded history the Egyptian civilization was dependent on the land inundated by the annual overflow of the Nile River. Outside this cultivatable region which fed the nation was the barren inhospitable desert. Construction of the Aswan Dam substituted commercial fertilizers for the age-old cycle of annual floods which sustained the fertility of the soil.

The total agricultural land in Egypt's 1,000,000 square kilometer area (386,000 square miles) is less than 39,000 square kilometers (15,000 square miles). The area of the Nile Delta . . . is about 18,000 square kilometers (7,000 square miles). Its importance to the economy of the country can hardly be overstated.

The black thread of the Nile River winds its way north through an irrigated valley that has changed little in appearance for more than 6,000 years. (Sheffield, 1983)

Other ancient civilizations in different parts of the world, such as those in the Tigris-Euphrates and Indus valleys, were also spatially defined by river valley regions.

The city of Rome was divided by the emperor Servius Tullius into four districts, later into fourteen by Augustus. Ancient Rome and Carthage divided the western Mediterranean into two domains of military, commercial, and political dominance which fluctuated in size during several centuries of irreconcilable conflict. Julius Caesar's opening declaration in his *Commentaries on the Gallic War* that "all Gaul is divided into three parts" signifies a regional concept. Throughout its long history, Rome treated its many conquered territories as regions called provinces, districts, colonies, or by geographical names such as western Sicily, Sardinia, or Corsica.

The concept of regions has been associated with an extraterrestrial moral world as well as the physical earth. Aristotle conceived the universe divided into two conceptual regions: a "sub-lunar" region consisting of fire, air, earth, and water; and a "supra-lunar" region composed of a quintescent substance: the Ether. The first of these involving atmospheric space, the earth, and man was considered negative or "bad"; the second extraterrestrial region was regarded as positive and "good."

In the Middle Ages, fortified cities were separated by largely uninhabited regions that were often controlled by powers different from those ruling the city, or by brigands romanticized in the literary figure of Robin Hood. The Episcopal bishop's diocese or see, and the region of influence of Medieval missionary orders such as the Dominicans and Franciscans, conformed to no political or secular boundaries. The Crusades related to regions of religious faith rather than political states.

Conceptually, religion divided the afterlife into the two regions of heaven and hell. Westward exploration across the oceans from Europe to the new worlds of America could only refer to anticipated or unknown lands in general directional or vague regional terms.

Later, during the Industrial Revolution, a new set of commercially determined regions was added. It was from the geographical regions containing the necessary mineral and agricultural materials that the steam power and processed products of the new manufacturing plants were derived. Transportation costs determined how far from the source of raw materials the factories could be located, and how far the finished products could be distributed and remain profitable at a given price. The first category of regions was established by geography and geology, the second by economics and consumer demand.

Since the early days of the United States, the West has been a distinct region, differing from the rest of the country geographically, geologically, economically, culturally, and in almost every other way. And between the one hundredth meridian at about the middle of the nation and the eastern slopes of the Rocky Mountains, extending from Canada to Mexico, is a climatic region with an average annual rainfall that does not permit profitable farming without irrigation from the underlying Ogalala Aquifer. For several centuries, the Northeast was the preeminent industrial region of the nation until textile and other manufacturing plants moved to the South with its lower labor costs and cheaper land.

Some regional differences are being reduced these days by the equalizing influences of television and the other mass media of communication, national and international marketing, and widespread personal travel. But new technologies emerging from the modern scientific era have created new regions such as those relating to the disposal of nuclear and toxic wastes, pesticide contamination, electromagnetic interference, or the region of orbiting debris produced by missiles, space probes, and vehicles launched during the past 25 years.

Regions have existed since earliest times and will continue as an increasingly important concept. They best represent actual conditions in the real world, or areas intentionally delineated to resolve a problem or manage an activity that extends beyond governmental borders.

regional   Because they are so numerous and diverse, regions are cat-
categories egorized in various ways by different individuals and organi-
zations employing them for different purposes. For example, the French employed the regional concept in their establishment of administrative *préfectures*, whose size was determined by a day's journey on horseback. Recently, continental France has been divided into 21 regions for planning purposes (Figure 62, page 183). *The Grand Dictionnaire Encyclopédique Larousse* (1984) lists four types of regions: territorial, metropolitan urban, parts of the human body, and a literary or philosophical domain. Examples are given of regions used in connection with academic fields and operational activities: aeronautics (air traffic control), military history (fortification), astrophysics (solar, hydrogen), history (districts of Ancient Rome), geography (natural), military operations (air, ground, water), geometry (edge formed by curves), oceanography (water circulation).

In this book regions are categorized and discussed according to their general characteristics, purpose, type, quality, coverage, academic use, and their employment by civil government, private enterprise, and the military services. Most regions belong to several of these categories.

All regions meet the requirements of their definition in that they either represent natural conditions or situations, or delineate areas on the ground or in the air for purposes that do not require coincidence with particular features of the physical world. Illustrating the first of these two groups are regions showing geographical, geological, or other physical features of the earth (Figure 1, Physiographic Regions, page 11).*

Illustrating the second are regions delineated for administrative purposes, which often coincide with governmental boundaries rather than geographical features on the ground. An exceptionally clear example of regions delineated without reference to features on the ground are those that are desig-

---

*Descriptive information is provided for each figure in this book in the following order: title indicating subject matter; type of region; field or area of activity most closely involved; primary use; additional categorization when appropriate; source of information.

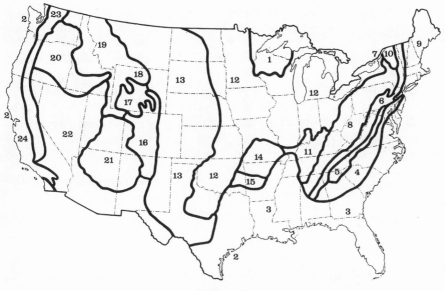

Figure 1

Legend

1. *Superior Upland*. Hilly area of erosional topography on ancient crystalline rocks. 2. *Continental Shelf*. Shallow, sloping submarine plain of sedimentation. 3. *Coastal Plain*. Low, hilly to nearly flat terraced plains on soft sediments. 4. *Piedmont province*. Gentle to rough, hilly terrain on belted crystalline rocks becoming more hilly toward mountains. 5. *Blue Ridge Province*. Mountains of crystalline rock 900 to 1800 mm (3000 to 6000 ft) high, mostly rounded summits. 6. *Valley and Ridge province*. Long mountain ridges and valleys eroded into strong and weak folded rock strata. 7. *St. Lawrence Valley*. Rolling lowlands with local rock hills. 8. *Appalachian Plateaus*. Generally steep-sided plateaus on sandstone bedrock, 900 to 1500 (3000 to 5000 ft) high on the east side, declining gradually to the west. 9. *New England province*. Rolling, hilly, erosional topography on crystalline rocks in the southeastern part, changing to high mountainous country in the central and northern parts. 10. *Adirondack province*. Subdued mountains on ancient crystalline rocks rising to more than 1500 m. 11. *Interior Low Plateaus*. Low plateaus on stratified rocks. 12. *Central Lowland*. Mostly low, rolling landscape and nearly level plains. Most of area covered by veneer of glacial deposits, including ancient lake beds and hilly, lake-dotted moraines. 13. *Great Plains*. Broad river plains and low plateaus on weak, stratified sedimentary rocks. Rises toward Rocky Mountains, reaching altitudes above 1800 m at some places. 14. *Ozark Plateaus*. High, hilly landscape on stratified rocks. 15. *Ouachita province*. Ridges and valleys eroded on upturned, folded strata. 16. *Southern Rocky Mountains*. Complex mountains rising to more than 4300m—(14,000 ft). 17. *Wyoming Basin*. Elevated plains and plateaus on sedimentary strata. 18. *Middle Rocky Mountains*. Complex mountains with

many intermontane basins and plains. 19. *Northern Rocky Mountains*. Rugged mountains with narrow intermontane basins. 20. *Columbia Plateau*. High rolling plateaus underlain by extensive lava flows; trenched by canyons. 21. *Colorado Plateau*. High plateaus on stratified rocks cut by deep canyons. 22. *Basin and Range province*. Mostly isolated ranges separated by wide desert plains. Many lakes, ancient lake beds, and alluvial fans. 23. *Cascade-Sierra Nevada Mountains*. The Sierra Nevada, in the southern part of the province, are high mountains eroded from crystalline rocks. The Cascades, in the northern part of the province, are high volcanic mountains. 24. *Pacific Border province*. Mostly very young, steep mountains; includes the extensive river plains in California.

PHYSIOGRAPHIC REGIONS
Intranational
Geography, Engineering
Descriptive
Reference: Press, Frank and Raymond Siever, EARTH. Copyright © 1974, 1978, 1982, 1986 (W. H. Freeman and Company), Third Edition, San Francisco, CA, 1982, p. 486. Used by permission.

nated for the control of air traffic below 18,000 feet altitude. They are drawn to equalize the density of air traffic directed by each regional control center, rather than the configuration or features of the earth's surface below. (Figure 2, Low Altitude Air Traffic Control, page 13)

Regional boundaries are most often linear, such as those for administrative purposes referred to in the previous paragraph and others that can be designated precisely (Figure 3, Major Salt Deposits, page 14). Some regions have indefinite zonal boundaries that have no precise linear termination but merge gradually into the surrounding space, such as those depicting meteorological and climatic regions, or the oceanographic expanse occupied by the Gulf Stream off the east coast of the United States (Figure 4, Climatic Zones, page 15).

purposes   Most of the regions illustrated in this book were formulated to identify or describe certain areas, conditions, situations, or *information* other particular information. Such a descriptive region unusually shaped, discontinuous in part, and extending over about one-half of the United States is illustrated in Figure 5, Heavy Soil Erosion Damage, page 16. Some regions are selected to *analysis* expand analytic understanding. The decennial census taken by

Figure 2
LOW ALTITUDE AIR TRAFFIC CONTROL
Intranational
Public Administration, Business Management
Operational
Reference: *IFR Wall Planning Chart*-East-West, Washington, DC (National Ocean Service, National Oceanic and Atmospheric Administration, U.S. Department of Commerce), 3 July to 28 August 1986.

the U.S. Bureau of the Census is tabulated by region, as well as nationally, by state, metropolitan areas, census districts, and in other ways. Figure 6a, U.S. Census: Analysis, on page 17, displays the regional tabulation of census data that best serves the great diversity of analytical uses for census information.

The Bureau of the Census also exemplifies the use of several *operations* operational regions by a single agency. Its subdivision of the continental United States into regions and districts within regions differs from those designated for the other two operational activities of this important federal agency supplying population statistics used for so many purposes. Figure 6b, U.S. Census: Operations, on page 18, shows two sets of regions: those delineated for decentralized operations, and the slightly different regions for providing the public with informational services.

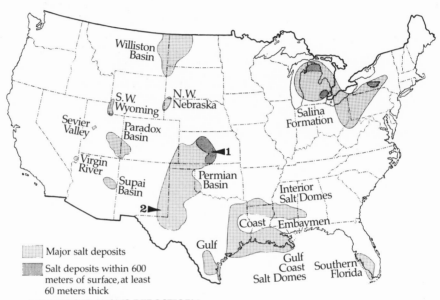

Williston
Basin

S.W.
Wyoming

N.W.
Nebraska

Salina
Formation

Sevier
Valley

Paradox
Basin

Virgin
River

Supai
Basin

Permian
Basin

Interior
Salt Domes

Còast   Embaymen

Gulf

Gulf
Coast   Southern
Salt Domes   Florida

Major salt deposits

Salt deposits within 600
meters of surface, at least
60 meters thick

1 PROPOSED LYONS REPOSITORY
2 POSSIBLE SITE FOR PROPOSED PILOT REPOSITORY

Figure 3
MAJOR SALT DEPOSITS
Intranational
Geology, Engineering
Descriptive
Dispersed
Reference: Keller, Edward J., *Environmental Geology*, Second Edition,
Columbus, OH (Merrill), 1979, p. 303.

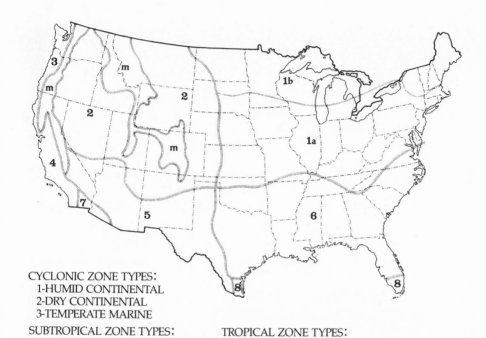

CYCLONIC ZONE TYPES:
  1-HUMID CONTINENTAL
  2-DRY CONTINENTAL
  3-TEMPERATE MARINE

SUBTROPICAL ZONE TYPES: TROPICAL ZONE TYPES:
  4-MEDITERRANEAN SUBTROPICAL   7-ARID TROPICAL
  5-DRY SUBTROPICAL   8-MONSOON TROPICAL
  6-HUMID SUBTROPICAL   m-HIGHLAND CLIMATES UNDIFFERENTIATED

Figure 4
CLIMATIC ZONES
Intranational
Meteorology
Descriptive
Indefinite Boundaries
Reference: National Resources Committee, *Regional Factors in National Planning*, Washington, DC (Government Printing Office), December 1935, p. 171.

Exceeds five tons per acre per year.

Figure 5
HEAVY SOIL EROSION DAMAGE
Intranational
Agricultural Science
Descriptive
Reference: Charlier, Marj., "Cropland Erosion Is a Growing Problem,"
The Wall Street Journal, 26 April 1986, p. 6. Reference: Soil Conservation
Service, U.S. Department of Agriculture.

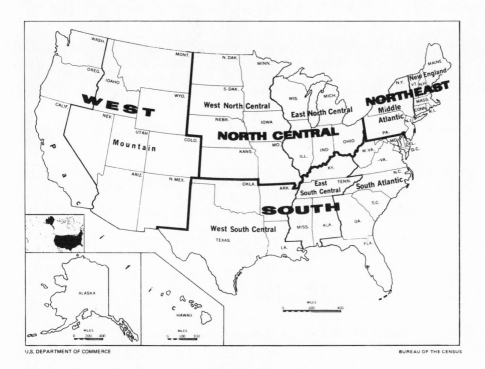

Figure 6a
U.S. CENSUS: ANALYSIS
Intranational
Demography
Analytical
Reference: Bureau of the Census, U.S. Census, U.S. Department of
Commerce, 1986.

Figure 6b
U.S. CENSUS: OPERATIONS
Intranational
Demography
Operational
Reference: Bureau of the Census, U.S. Department of Commerce, 1986.

The background economic information on manufacturing and employment in The Netherlands developed by the central government is another example of descriptive regional data, needed for many quantitative purposes relating to facilities and services, or resource allocation directed at equalizing economic conditions among the various regions of the country. (Figure 7a,b,c, pages 20, 21)

research   Some regions are designed for research. The Arctic region in Figure 8, Arctic Environment, page 22, is designated for an intercontinental investigation, sponsored by the United States, of the long-range effects of the physical conditions and forces unique to the polar environment. This region generates much of the world's weather and affects global climates. Furthermore, it is an area of great environmental sensitivity; a small change in temperature within the region could increase the rate at which the arctic ice is melting and in time raise the level of the oceans sufficiently to submerge coastal areas around the world. It is in these coastal areas that many of the world's cities and a significant percentage of its productive activity are located.

Other regions provide organizations of all types with a spatial basis for decentralized administration, rather than operational management centralized in a single national headquarters. This may involve responsibility for a single function such as flood control or health services by civil government, military command of a regional area, or sales, product distribution, and customer-client service by a private nonprofit organization. An example of the latter is the regional organization of the American Association of Retired Persons serving its membership of several million members (Figure 9, page 23). *administration*

Authority for all of the activities of a civil government, military service, or business enterprise within a designated area may be delegated to a regional executive or governing body subject only to certain policy directives and limitations on capital expenditure set by higher authority. This is the case with multiple-purpose regions established by civil government, operational areas for decentralized business management, or the regions into which the world has been divided for the unified command of all military forces within the region. Illustrating each of these in succession are: Figure 26a, Tennessee Valley Authority, page 52; Figure 51, Production, Distribution, Sales: *The Wall Street Journal*, page 143; and Figure 10, U.S. Unified Global Military Commands, page 24.

The world and nations may also be divided into regions for purely planning purposes. Private enterprises study present and potential competition in the market areas or regions where they operate or would like to expand. The military services maintain contingency plans for various military and political situations in different parts of the world. Civil governments plan the current operations and possible enlargement of the regional areas served by the many special service districts. *planning*

As would be expected in view of their many uses, there are different types of regions. A dispersed region represents characteristics that are distributed throughout the area uniformly, irregularly, randomly, or concentrated at particular places, as the case may be, but these characteristics are not convergent or dependent on a single predominant point in space. Most *types* *dispersed*

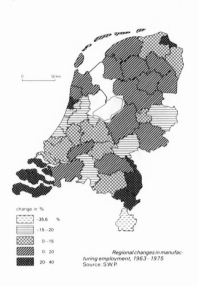

change in %

-35,6   %

-15--20

0--15

0- 20

20- 40

*Regional changes in manufac-
turing employment, 1963 - 1975
Source: S.W.P.*

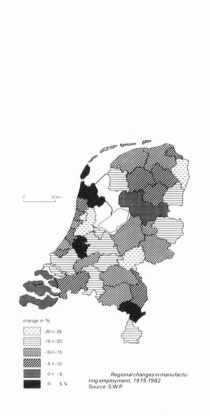

change in %

-20 <-25

-15 <-20

-10 <-15

-5 <-10

0 < -5

0-   5 %

*Regional changes in manufactu-
ring employment, 1975-1982
Source: S.W.P.*

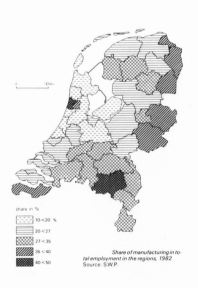

share in %

10 <20   %

20 <27

27 <35

35 < 40

40 < 50

*Share of manufacturing in to-
tal employment in the regions, 1982
Source: S.W.P.*

Figure 7a
**MANUFACTURING EMPLOYMENT, THE NETHERLANDS:
CHANGE 1963–75**
Intranational
Economics, Public Administration
Descriptive
Reference: Meijer, Henk (Editor), *i.d.g. bulletin*, 1983/84,
Utrecht/The Hague, 1984, p. 36.

Figure 7b
**MANUFACTURING EMPLOYMENT, THE NETHERLANDS:
CHANGE 1975–82**
Intranational
Economics, Public Administration
Descriptive
Reference: Meijer, Henk (Editor, *i.d.g. bulletin*, 1983/84,
Utrecht/The Hague, 1984, p. 36.

Figure 7c
**MANUFACTURING EMPLOYMENT, THE NETHERLANDS:
SHARE 1982**
Intranational
Economics, Public Administration
Descriptive
Reference: Meijer, Henk (Editor), *i.d.g. bulletin*, 1983/84,
Utrecht/The Hague, 1984, p. 36.

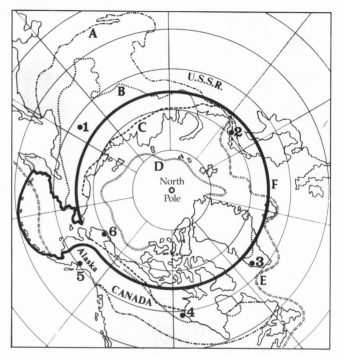

---·· **A** Continuous Permafrost ···· **B** Discontinuous Permafrost ---**C** Treeline
ⅢⅢ **D** Minimum Pack Ice Extent ·ⅲ·ⅲ· **E** Maximum Pack Ice Extent
━ **F** Artic Boundary (defined by 1984 Artic Research and Policy Act)
1 Yakutsk **2** Murmansk **3** Nuuk **4** Barrow **5** Anchorage **6** Churchill

Figure 8
ARCTIC ENVIRONMENT
Intercontinental
Meteorology, Geography, Biology
Descriptive
Reference: Washburn, A. L., and Gunter Weller, "Arctic Research in the
National Interest," *Science*, 8 August 1986, p. 634.

Figure 9
AMERICAN ASSOCIATION OF RETIRED PERSONS
Intranational
Business Management
Operational
Reference: *Modern Maturity*, August-September, 1986, p. 16.

ADCOM : Aerospace Defense Command
(NORAD) : North American Air Defense
LANTCOM : Atlantic Command

SOUTHCOM : South Command
EUCOM : European Command
CENTCOM : Central Command
PACOM : Pacific Command

Note: Whether or not there is a boundary between EUCOM and PACOM through the Soviet Union
is classified information. Mexico is outside the jurisdiction of any U.S. unified or specified command.

Figure 10
U.S. UNIFIED GLOBAL MILITARY COMMANDS
Global, Intercontinental, Continental
Military Science
Operational
References: Collins, John M., *U.S.-Soviet Military Balance, Concepts and
Capabilities, 1960–1980*, New York (McGraw-Hill), 1980, p. 59.
Commander David L. Dillon, Director, Navy Office of Information, Los
Angeles, California: Personal Communication, 1986.

geographical regions represent physical features that are distributed throughout the designated area without a single convergent focus.

nodal   By comparison, a nodal region contains a central or most
influential activity or feature that is the focus for the surrounding region or otherwise the dominant force within it. It is an
area of directly related effects that emanate from a determina-
tive point. An environmental delineation of the dispersion of
acid rain or other contamination from a single or several adjacent sources illustrates a nodal region. The radioactive fallout
from the explosion at the Chernobyl nuclear power plant in the

Soviet Union on 26 April 1986 formed a nodal region of discontinuous parts extending throughout Europe and across the
globe (Figures 11a,b, Contamination, Radioactive Fallout, pages
26, 27). As indicated previously, regions selected for air traffic
control are nodal, since their form and extent are determined
by the directive capacity of the control center. Metropolitan
regions are nodal by definition, since they reflect the extent to
which the central city influences the conditions or operations
of surrounding municipalities, unincorporated areas, and outlying rural countryside.

    There are no fixed immutable regions in an absolute sense.   *fixed*
Everything in the world is changing or subject to change. Even
as seemingly fixed a region as an area on the earth within a
circle of exact radius drawn from a cartographically precise point,
is subject to very gradual change caused by the minute movement of the underlying tectonic plates forming the earth's surface. Despite this theoretical exclusion, there are fixed regions
for practical and planning purposes. Geological regions defining precisely identifiable natural resources or administrative
regions with exact boundaries are examples. In the short term,
many physiographic regions are subject only to minor adjust-
ments brought about by erosion, slight shifting of water courses,
or some other relatively small change in a natural feature comprising a regional border. When boundaries are not subject to
significant unintentional change for years, administrative regions
can be considered fixed for almost all the uses to which they
are put.

    There are regions which are indeterminate because of shift-   *indeterminate*
ing boundaries. Meteorological regions important for many
purposes change constantly as shown every day in newspaper
and television weather reports employing aerial photographs
taken from orbiting satellites (Figure 12, Weather Forecast, page
28). The extent of the ocean area subject to the irregular ocean
current El Niño off the coast of Peru—an important element
of global climate and source of agricultural fertilizer made from
the anchovy catch—varies from year to year depending on
oceanographic and meteorological circumstances not yet fully
understood. "Experts rank El Niño as the number one force
disturbing world climate patterns. . . . ." (Canby, 1984). The

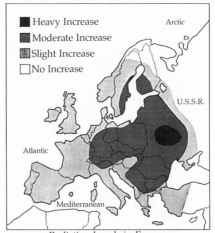

Radiation Levels in Europe
Compared with Normal Levels : 3 May 1986

Figure 11a
CONTAMINATION, RADIOACTIVE FALLOUT: EUROPE
Continental
Meteorology, Medicine
Descriptive
Indefinite, Changing
Reference: Hudson, Richard L., "Lingering Fallout, A Year Later, Mishap
at Chernobyl Damps Atom-Power Industry," *The Wall Street Journal*,
23 April 1987, p. 24.

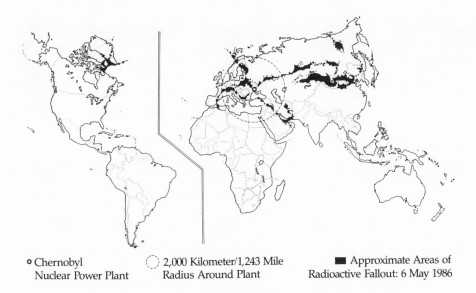

| ° Chernobyl
Nuclear Power Plant | ◌ 2,000 Kilometer/1,243 Mile
Radius Around Plant | ■ Approximate Areas of
Radioactive Fallout: 6 May 1986 |

Figure 11b
CONTAMINATION, RADIOACTIVE FALLOUT: GLOBAL
Global, Intercontinental, Continental
Meteorology, Medicine
Descriptive
Indefinite, Changing, Dispersed
Reference: Hohenemser, C., M. Deicher, A. Ernst, H. Hofsass, G. Linder,
and E. Recknagel, "Chernobyl: An Early Report," *Environment*, June 1986,
pp. 6, 7, 11.

Metropolitan Forecast

Today will be mostly sunny in the New York metropolitan area. High temperatures will be between 63 and 67 degrees. Tonight will be clear and cool, with low temperatures between 45 and 50 degrees. Mostly sunny skies are forecast tomorrow. High temperatures will be between 65 and 70 degrees.

Regional Forecast

New York City	New Jersey
Today: Mostly sunny. High: 63-67. Northeasterly winds at 15 miles per hour. Tonight: Mostly clear. Low: 45-50. Tomorrow: Mostly sunny. High: 65-70.	Today: Mostly sunny. High: 63-67. Northeasterly winds at 15 m.p.h. Tonight: Mostly clear. Low: 45-50. Tomorrow: Mostly sunny. High: 65-70.

Long Island	Connecticut
Today: Mostly sunny. High: 60-65. Northeasterly winds at 15 to 20 m.p.h. Tonight: Mostly clear. Low: 40-45. Tomorrow: Mostly sunny. High: 63-67.	Today: Partly sunny. High: 60-65. Northeasterly winds at 15 m.p.h. Tonight: Mostly clear. Low: 35-40. Tomorrow: Mostly sunny. High: 65-70.

Westchester, Rockland	Extended Forecast
Today: Mostly sunny. High: 60-65. Northeasterly winds at 15 m.p.h. Tonight: Mostly clear. Low: 33-37. Tomorrow: Mostly sunny. High: 63-67.	Sunday: Mostly fair. Monday: Mostly fair. Tuesday: Mostly fair. Temperatures: Daytime highs will average in the upper 60's while overnight lows will average in the 50's throughout the period.

Reservoirs   By New York City Department of Environmental Protection

New York and Westchester:
Water level on May 7: 98.9%   Consumption: 1.241 billion gallons.
Estimated normal: 100%   Mayor's goal: 1.100 billion gallons.

National Forecast

8 P.M., E.D.T.
Friday
May 9, 1986

Numbers in circles show highest and lowest projected barometer readings, 29.92 is normal

Showers and heavy thunderstorms will stretch from the upper Mississippi Valley across western Iowa and Missouri to the Southern Plains States. Rain, changing to snow in the high elevations, will extend from the central interior mountain region to the northern and central Rockies. Rain and showers will be scattered in North Dakota and the Pacific Northwest. High temperatures will range from the 40's in the Rockies to the 80's in California.

Figure 12
WEATHER FORECAST
Intranational, Interstate
Meteorology
Descriptive
Flexible, Indefinite
Reference: *The New York Times*, 9 May 1986, p. D23. Copyright © 1986 by
the New York Times Company. Reprinted by permission.

indefinite ocean region affected by El Niño is also indefinite in that it does not occur regularly. (Figure 13, Physical Regions of the Oceans, D, on page 30)

Although subject to unexpected change, identification of climatic zones such as those shown in Figure 4 on page 15 has been considered essential for agricultural and many other purposes since earliest times. The region of devastating drought in the southeastern United States displays the weather situation as it existed for a very brief time (Figure 14, Drought in the Southeast, 17 July 1986, page 31). This climatic anomaly is *temporary* therefore a temporary region. The fallout from the Chernobyl disaster, referred to previously, comprised a region that was temporary in its shorter-lived radioactive effects, and of unknown duration for the longer-lived components of the radiation.

Regions containing diurnal, seasonal, or other periodic phenomena can be categorized as fluctuating. For example, a *fluctuating* regional representation of demand for electricity within the economical distribution area of a generating plant would show the different boundaries for residential, commercial, and industrial demands: between day and night, between different seasons of the year, and under prevailing climatic variations. Or a regional representation by civil government of a flood plain would indicate the different areas inundated during different seasons, weather, and other contributing conditions within the watershed that have occurred periodically in the past and can be expected in the future. Strategic studies formulated to plan a military campaign should show any physical and environmental fluctuations within the region involved that could affect the operation.

Not all regions enclose continuous space within their boundaries. Discontinuous regions consist of integral parts that *discontinuous* are not contiguous comprising a continuous area but are separated in space. Figure 15, Underground Water Resources, page 32, shows the locations of subterranean aquifers in the United States. Although they are found separately at different locations in the country, they constitute a single regional resource with respect to national policies, plans, and legislation concerning water supply, water use, and actual and potential contamination.

> From California to Florida, the nation's ground water, a vast unseen resource beneath the earth's surface, is far more polluted by a greater number of contaminants than previously believed. The more authorities sample underground water, the more they are finding toxic chemicals, pesticides, and other possibly hazardous substances. According to growing consensus among authorities in government, industry, and environmental groups, the trend indicates a serious environmental problem that merits national attention. (Sun, 1986)

Similarly, the underground salt formations depicted in Figure 3, Major Salt Deposits, page 14, constitute a single discontinuous region of potential depositories for the underground

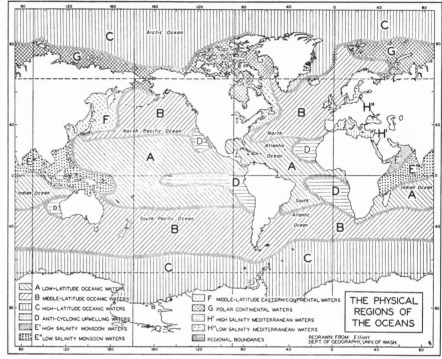

Physical Regions of the Oceans, by Elliott.

Figure 13
PHYSICAL REGIONS OF THE OCEANS
Global, Intercontinental
Oceanographic
Descriptive
Flexible, Indefinite
Reference: James, Preston E. and Clarence F. Jones (Editors), *American
Geography: Inventory and Prospect*, Syracuse, NY (Published for the
Association of American Geographers by Syracuse University Press),
1954, p. 420.

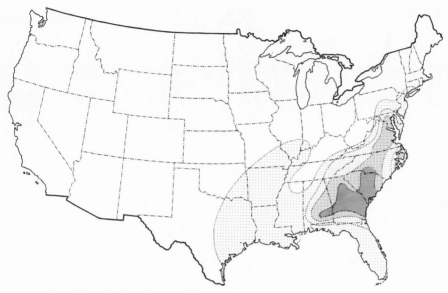

☒ EXTREME: Too dry for plants to exist

☐ EXCESSIVE: Plant growth retarded

▒ SEVERE: Plants likely to wilt

░ ABNORMAL: Not ideal moisture, but plant growth continues

Figure 14
DROUGHT IN THE SOUTHEAST: 17 JULY 1986*
Interstate, Intranational
Meteorology, Economics
Temporary

*Dryness measured by a government agricultural weather facility reflecting the amount of moisture available in a five-foot-deep soil sample.

Reference: *The New York Times*, 17 July 1986, p. Y9.

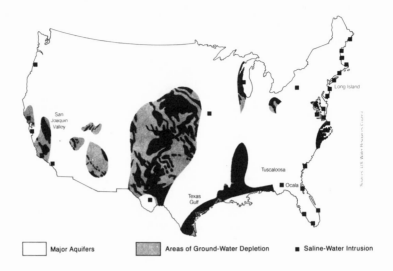

| Major Aquifers | Areas of Ground-Water Depletion | ■ Saline-Water Intrusion |

Figure 15
UNDERGROUND WATER RESOURCES
Intranational, Interstate
Geology
Descriptive
Dispersed
Reference: Miller, G. Tyler, Jr., *Living in the Environment*, Belmont, CA
(Wadsworth), Third Edition, 1979, p. 269. Copyright © by Wadsworth,
Inc. Used by permission.

storage of highly radioactive nuclear waste with a half-life of
many years to several centuries. These spatially separate geological formations must be considered as a single entity in order
to decide how the national need for nuclear waste disposal sites
is to be met, despite the attitude of individual states that the
sites selected be "somewhere else."

The government has considered disposal of radioactive
waste in salt since 1955, and during 1966 and 1967 it initiated the Project Salt Vault in which high level solid-waste
disposal procedures were simulated in abandoned salt mines
. . . [one of which] would eventually become the National
Radioactive Waste Repository. (Keller, 1979)

From these examples it is clear that whether or not regions are discontinuous depends not only on the nature of the information presented but also on how large an area is involved. Regions depicting the water resources or salt formation in a single state would not be discontinuous if only one underground aquifer or salt formation exists within the state.

Warm and cold air fronts, pressure areas, high altitude jet *flexible* streams, and other atmospheric phenomena constitute the world's weather. These meteorological regions are flexible in that they "adapt themselves readily to changes of shape." Although they change continually, they maintain their primary characteristics, permitting the weather forecasts that are crucial to many human activities ranging from global air travel and agricultural production to local construction schedules and individual family plans.

Since acid rain and radioactive fallout are airborne and therefore subject to weather conditions, these regions of air pollution are flexible. Their borders are zonal rather than linear. The ground area involved at any given time is changing continually, although there are areas of maximum and average ground coverage. The area subject to radioactive fallout from the Chernobyl nuclear disaster in the Soviet Union in 1986 shown in Figure 11b on page 27, is a flexible region of nonconcentric, irregular, and attenuated pollution carried far and wide by global winds.

The landing of astronauts on the moon involved an unusual operational region of considerable complexity: a flexible volume of space extending between the earth and the moon. The 475,000-mile round trip was conceived, planned, and executed within a spatial envelope that varies continually as the earth and moon constantly change their positions relative to each other. Not only does the moon revolve around the earth in an elliptical orbit at 66 miles per second but the earth is rotating at 0.3 miles per second in its orbit around the sun, continually exposing a different face to the moon. Fortunately for space travel between the two, their relative positions are precisely predictable.

For years, federal agencies have selected operating regions that often vary only slightly one from another, sometimes more a matter of current or incidental preference than need or adequate justification. Within the U.S. Department of Agriculture there are thirty or more units with different operating regions. The federal government concludes that such regional diversity makes it more difficult and costly to correlate data gathered by different agencies and relating to different areas. Cooperative action between agencies with different operating regions may also be more difficult when their headquarters are also located in different cities. Accordingly:

standard   Standard federal administrative regions have been established . . . to achieve greater uniformity in the location and geographic jurisdiction of federal field offices. . . . Agencies are now required to adopt the uniform system when new offices are established. (National Archives of the United States, 1982) (Figure 16, Standard Federal Regions, page 35)

quality   The quality or validity of regions used for descriptive, analytical, or research purposes depends of course on the reliability of the underlying information and the accuracy with which it is measured and depicted in the regional representation. Good quality requires application of accepted standards of careful investigation, proper statistical evaluation, correct presentation of data and conclusions, and an indication of the degree of accuracy or percentage significance of the results.

The validity of a region used for planning purposes also depends on reliable underlying data and their proper processing. Another indication of regional quality is the successful functioning of the operation that was the objective and reason for the establishment of the planning region in the first place. As discussed later in Chapter 3, the operation may be a single-function district or region providing a product or service, a multiple-purpose river basin development involving several related functions, or comprehensive planning of the principal components of the organism.

coverage   Regions vary greatly in the area they include within their boundaries, with a lower limit indicated in the definition dis-
outer space cussed on page 6. The largest regions are in outer space. Dividing the heavens into northern and southern hemispheres for observational and record-keeping purposes establishes the two largest astronomical regions: each encompassing one-half

Figure 16
STANDARD FEDERAL REGIONS
Intranational
Public Administration
Operational
Reference: *The United States Directory of Federal Regional Structure,
1981–1982*, Washington DC (The National Archives of the United States),
p. 1.

an infinity of celestial space. Numerous astronomical regions have been identified for various purposes: the Milky Way describing our galaxy extending over 1,000 light years of space; the circumsolar region affected most directly by the sun; technical regions such as chromospheres and magnetospheres identifying celestial regions of light and electrical force; H1 and H2 regions of ionized and neutral hydrogen.

The nearby regions of the Milky Way offer abundant evidence that star formation is an ongoing process. . . . And yet, despite years of searching, astronomers have never been able to catch an embryonic star at the moment of formation. . . . The star that finally ended the search was . . . detected . . . in the Rho Ophiuchi molecular cloud just north of the bright star Antares in the constellation of Scorpius. The Rho Ophiuchi region is well studied. (Waldrop, 1986)

An amateur astronomer . . . had seen the eruption [of the supernova 1987A] while scanning for variable stars and supernovas in the region of 30 Doradus, a huge region of ionized gas and active star formation located in the [Large Megellanic] Cloud. (Waldrop, 1987)

The troposphere is a very large region encircling the earth from five to eleven miles above its surface. The stratosphere extends into outer space for another forty miles. Both of these regions are involved in the "greenhouse effect": the atmospheric buildup of carbon dioxide and other gases primarily from the burning of fossil fuels that slows the escape of heat from the earth's surface.

Scientists and senators at a hearing by the Environmental Pollution subcommittee agreed that the dangers of manmade changes in the atmosphere had moved from hypothesis to imminent reality and must be addressed quickly.

They said the rise in temperatures was expected to cause profound climatic changes and raise sea levels substantially.

Witnesses at the hearing also testified that the ozone layer in the upper atmosphere, which protects the earth from the sun's ultraviolet light, was being rapidly depleted by manmade gases, and that the increased radiation would result in a rise in skin cancer cases and other ecological damage. (Shabecoff, 1986)

near
outer space   Orbiting satellites, space stations, and space vehicles have introduced new considerations and new concerns in near outer space.

There is no code of law specifically governing routine transportation systems like the Space Shuttle. With the prospect of major commercial ventures in space looming large, some thought is now being given to the expected volume of traffic to and from orbit. . . .

One common source of debate is the height at which Earth's atmosphere ends and outer space begins. . . . what should be the distinction between a country's sovereign air space and the *res communis* beyond? (Christol, 1984)

An unanticipated region affecting space travel has been created in recent years. It illustrates the advent of new regions as science identifies new substances and forces, technology produces new products, and humans engage in new activities.

At present, more than 5,600 man-made objects are tracked in orbit around the Earth. Of these, about 72 percent are classed as debris (a category that does not include dead satellites). . . . It includes spent rocket stages, ejected satellite shrouds, clamps, exploded fuel tanks, insulation, and odds and ends left by astronauts.

In addition to these relatively large objects, there are reckoned to be tens of thousands of pieces of untracked debris the size of marbles, and literally billions of paint flakes orbiting Earth. There are also transient bits of frozen sewage from the shuttle. . . .

Even a tiny 0.5-mm metal chip, encountered at the average collision speed in space of 10 kilometers a second [22,369 miles per hour] can puncture a space suit, if it hits at the right point, and kill an astronaut. Objects 1 to 10 millimeters across [4 to 40 one-hundredths of an inch] can damage a spacecraft. . . .

Once a critical density is reached, the pollution will grow at an exponential rate. . . . the net balance of junk in space is growing by 300 to 500 objects per year. . . . A small, marble-like object released in a circular orbit at 500 kilometers [311 miles] would stay aloft for about a year. But if it were released at 800 kilometers [497 miles], it would stay up for 30 years. And at 1,200 kilometers [746 miles] it would remain in space 300 years. (Marshall, 1985)

Nearly 3,000 pounds of radioactive debris is orbiting in a region selected as a nuclear dump, about 600 miles above Earth. (*The New York Times*, 1986)

The world is divided into very large regions of global sig- *global* nificance. They are receiving more attention since high altitude photography and remote sensing from earth resources satellites provide aerial views and information concerning the earth's surface and subsurface previously unavailable. The result is greater awareness and understanding of global features and their relation to environmental conditions vital to human welfare and survival.

Among the most basic global regions are those represented by the tectonic plates of the lithosphere which underlie the earth's surface (Figure 17, Major Lithosphere Plates, page 38). Their gradual and inexorable movement relates to volcanic and earthquake activity at the earth's surface. The temperate and tropical latitudes constitute global regions since they are large bands around the earth with significant biological, geographical, and socioeconomic characteristics.

> Physiologically and behaviorally, each species in temperate regions must have an ecological amplitude sufficient to cope with radical seasonal changes in weather. While seasonal, most tropical climates fail to reach temperate extremes, and organisms adapted to them are correspondingly stenotopic. Such traits make tropical species more vulnerable to perturbation. (Patterson, 1986)

Desert areas stretching around most of the earth in the middle latitudes affect global weather and almost every aspect of human and other animal life within these regions. In Africa, the 3.5 million square miles of the Sahara Desert, occupying more than one–quarter of the land area of the continent, are creeping south and extending the region of heat and dryness without reference to national borders, but with far-reaching consequences for the countries being invaded and the economic and political stability of the entire continent (Figure 18, Deserts, Arid Regions, Potential Desert Areas, page 40).

> Dry areas cover about one-third of earth's landmass and support some 720 million people, a [seventh] of the world's population. And while climate created the deserts, it is Man who aids and abets their piecemeal advance across the boundaries between arid and temperate lands. Livestock overgrazes and tramples vegetation. Trees and woody plants are slashed for fuel. Marginal lands are cleared and plowed in desperate farming attempts. Improper irrigation sterilizes the earth with salt and alkali. And as desert-dwelling populations increase, productivity plummets. (Gore, 1979)

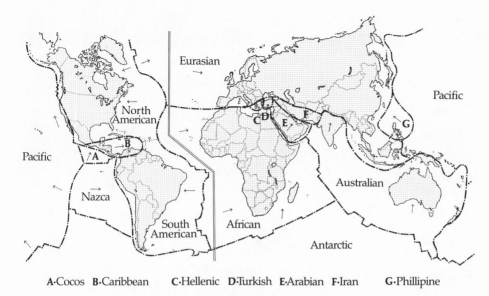

A·Cocos B·Caribbean   C·Hellenic D·Turkish E·Arabian F·Iran   G·Phillipine

Figure 17
MAJOR LITHOSPHERE PLATES
Global
Geology
Descriptive
Reference: Ludman, Allan, and Nicholas K. Coch, *Physical Geology*, New
York (McGraw-Hill), 1982, p. 474.

The dense tropical rain forests in South America, Africa,
Malaysia, Indonesia, and New Guinea are part of a global region
bordering the equator with special environmental characteristics. They may harbor many different species of plants, animals, and insects existing in different vertical strata extending
from the deeply shadowed forest floor to sunlit treetops several
hundred feet above. (Figure 19, Tropical Rain Forests, page 41)

In the closely woven tangle of vines and tree branches
dwell snakes, land crabs, rodents and other mammals,
insects and birds that know little of terra firma. There are
earthworms that never come to Earth and ground beetles
that would probably die on the ground. We know almost
nothing about this exotic world. (Coniff, 1986)

Continental South America comprises 12% of the world's
land area, yet its biotic resources are extraordinarily rich
. . .: it contains about 800 species of terrestrial mammals,

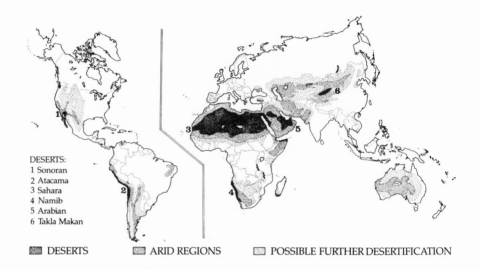

DESERTS:
1 Sonoran
2 Atacama
3 Sahara
4 Namib
5 Arabian
6 Takla Makan

▓ DESERTS   ▓ ARID REGIONS   ▒ POSSIBLE FURTHER DESERTIFICATION

Figure 18
DESERTS, ARID REGIONS, POTENTIAL DESERT AREAS
Global, Intercontinental, Intracontinental, International
Geography
Descriptive
Reference: Gore, Rick, "An Age-Old Challenge Grows," *National Geographic*, November 1979, pp. 604–606.

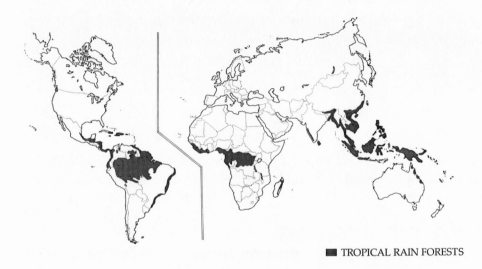

TROPICAL RAIN FORESTS

Figure 19
TROPICAL RAIN FORESTS
Global, Intercontinental, Intracontinental, International
Geography, Botany, Biology, Ecology
Descriptive
Reference: White, Peter T., "Nature's Dwindling Treasures, RAIN
FOREST," *National Geographic*, January 1983, pp. 10–11.

19% of the world total; approximately 90,000 species of flowering plants are found there (more than one-third of the world total); less than a square mile of forest in Colombia's Choco may support more than 1,100 species of trees; a hectare or less of forest in the Brazilian Amazon supports more than 500 species of trees and shrubs. . . .

The flora and fauna of South America are recognized as resources not only to the continent, but to the world. . . . Generally, the Neotropics are viewed as a biosphere resource because they may harbor innumerable food and drug resources, possible biocides, and other products that could be of great use. . . . The region is also extremely important to global weather and biogeochemical cycles, such as those of carbon, air, and oxygen. (Maris, 1986)

If these forests are eliminated—as seems likely at the present rate of deforestation to provide timber and open up the land for agriculture and grazing—the world will suffer a major loss. Efforts are being made to reduce the rapid rate of destruction and preserve as many large regions of tropical rain forest as possible.

After a 10-year campaign, a 450-mile-long ribbon of Atlantic forests covering 3.3 million acres of São Paulo State was declared a protected national landmark, raising hopes that hundreds of endangered animal species and thousands of plant species can be saved from extinction.

In addition, negotiations are under way to extend the classification to the entire 1,200-mile Serra do Mar mountain range where, thanks to steep slopes and hostile terrain, most of the 3 percent of the surviving Atlantic forests are situated.

"This is the first time in Latin America that an entire region has been protected. . . ."

There are other signs of rising environmental awareness in Brazil. The country's new civilian government has for the first time created a Cabinet-level ministry with responsibility for the environment. . . . (Riding, 1985)

Other regions of large size but of less than global scale extend
intercontinental between continents. The largest of these is probably the mon-

soon region covering most of middle Africa, northern Mada-gascar, India, China, Korea, Japan, the Philippines, south-eastern Asia, Indonesia, New Guinea, and the northern tip of Australia (Figure 20, Monsoon, page 43). Almost three billion people—three-fifths of the world's population—live in this intercontinental region agriculturally dependent on the sea-sonal rains of the monsoon. If the rains are delayed for several months, severe drought can ensue in east Africa and other regions. In many places the advent of the monsoon rains brings widespread flooding and damage.

How well Asia eats largely depends on the monsoon. The most densely populated countries on earth rely on the monsoon for most of their annual rainfall—and on rainfall for the success of their agricultural economies.

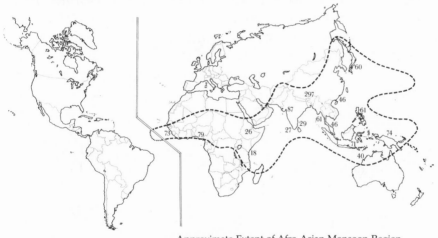

---- Approximate Extent of Afro-Asian Monsoon Region

Figure 20
MONSOON*
Intercontinental, Intracontinental, International
Meteorology, Economics
Descriptive

*Numbers indicate the average rainfall in inches during the peak season at various locations throughout the monsoon region. Peak season is from June to August, except in Malaysia, Philippines, Indonesia, and Australia when it is from December to February, and in East Africa from March to May.

Reference: Vesilind, Prut J., "Life Birth of Half the World, MONSOONS," *National Geographic*, December 1984, pp. 116–117.

But perhaps no country is as dependent on the monsoon as India. About 70% of India's labor force is farmers, three-quarters of the population lives on farms and 60% of India's food is produced during the summer rains—the southwest monsoon. Half of India's manufacturing and trading are agriculture-based, and a third of the nation's energy comes from rivers replenished by the monsoon.

"Monsoon is the life and blood of India. . . ." (Kronholz, 1986)

The Arctic region referred to previously on page 22 as an example of a large area established for research purposes, is intercontinental in scope, involving northern portions of Alaska, the United States, and Europe-Asia. Two of the regions for unified global command of the U.S. military services are intercontinental. PACOM includes Australia and eastern Asia, EUCOM parts of Europe-Asia and Africa (Figure 10, U.S. Unified Global Military Commands, page 24).

The area covered by regions decreases progressively as the scope of geographical consideration is narrowed, or the size of the organization or jurisdiction involved is reduced. In general, any larger unit is composed of smaller, more numerous components. Accordingly, regionalization increases as it is applied to successive components. Regional problems and needs are also more apparent as they are smaller in scale and closer by; for many people they have a greater reality and urgency than a larger region extending far away. As discussed in Chapter 3, regional planning covering smaller areas can be realized within the governmental jurisdiction containing them. Larger-scale regional planning requires cooperation between different governments, difficult to achieve under the best of circumstances.

The span of regional coverage ranges from vast regions having to do with outer space to those covering small local areas. Illustrations in this book which depict various kinds of regions also exemplify different areal coverage.

intracontinental   Some regions are intracontinental; for example, several in North America involve environmental pollutants.

The United States and Mexico have agreed to control emissions from copper smelters on both sides of the border. . . .

Under a second agreement on an environmental issue, Mexico pledged to deal with the raw sewage of Tijuana that is now pouring into the San Diego area at the rate of 13 million gallons a day.

The emissions of sulphur from the copper smelters, two of which are in Mexico and one in the United States, have been a potential source of acid rain. (*The New York Times*, 23 July 1985)

A comparable situation in northern Europe involves France, the low countries and Scandinavia, several eastern block countries, and the Soviet Union. Resolution of this atmospheric problem requires sufficient cooperation among the nations involved to balance the economic advantages of industrial facilities operating at least cost, providing employment and tax revenue, with the injurious effects of acid rain fallout on men and materials. This is the basic difficulty confronting almost all programs of environmental control or mitigation.

Norwegian scientists estimate that 16 tons of sulphur dioxide pollutants drift over from Britain each year and, after being converted into acids in the atmosphere, fall to earth, help to cause widespread plant and wildlife devastation, including the extinction of salmon in seven major rivers. . . . Other nations, particularly East Germany, have been found to be a large source of the poisonous sulphur emissions. East Germany, the Soviet Union and Czechoslovakia are pledged members of the 30 percent club . . . with the goal of a 30 percent reduction in the 1980 level of sulphur emissions by 1993. (Clines, 1986)

The operational regions for the air defense of North America are another example of intracontinental regions covering the United States and Canada (Figure 21, North American Air Defense (NORAD), page 46).

Arresting and reducing the pollution of the Rhine River in *international* Europe required years of effort. Its international drainage basin necessitated cooperative action between the four countries contributing to its condition: Switzerland, France, West Germany, and The Netherlands. Unfortunately, this achievement of the International Rhine Protection Commission was set back for an

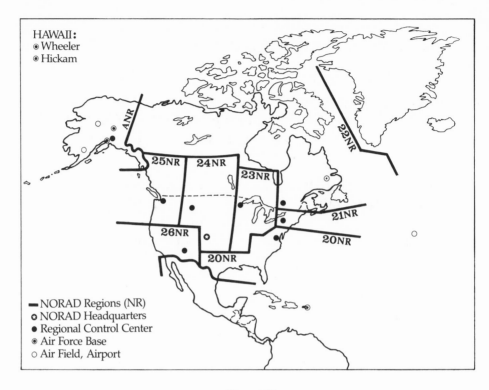

HAWAII:
⊕ Wheeler
⊕ Hickam

— NORAD Regions (NR)
⊙ NORAD Headquarters
● Regional Control Center
⊛ Air Force Base
○ Air Field, Airport

Figure 21
NORTH AMERICAN AIR DEFENSE (NORAD)
Intercontinental
Military Science
Operational
Reference: *U.S. War Machine*, An Encyclopedia of American Military
Equipment and Strategy, New York (Crown), 1983, p. 156.

estimated 10 years on 1 November 1986, when 30 tons of toxic
waste were discharged into the Rhine River as a consequence
of a fire at the warehouse of a large chemical corporation in
Basel, Switzerland.

> The . . . accident has dramatically illustrated the need for
> greater collaboration between countries where, because of
> their close proximity, a major accident in one can have
> dramatic consequences in several others.
>   "For many years, the danger of trans-frontier accidents
> has not been considered urgent, since there have been
> very few of them. . . . Everyone knew they could take place,
> but the possibility was largely ignored; now we have a
> dramatic illustration of what can happen." (Dickson, 1986)

Most of the major rivers of the world—such as the Nile, Amazon, Indus, or Orinoco—have regional drainage basins that include more than one nation. The River Blindness Control Program in northern Africa includes five nations in the first phase and two more in the second (Figure 22, Onchocerciasis (River Blindness) Control Program, page 48).

> . . .[the disease] now impairs or destroys the sight of 40 million people in Africa and South America, scientists report. River blindness, or onchocerciasis, is caused by a parasite that is spread from person to person by blackflies that breed in rivers and streams. (*The New York Times*, September 1986)

The descriptive geographic regions to be taken into account in military actions in Europe extend across many different nations (Figure 23, Military Geographic Regions, page 49).

The Mississippi, Missouri, and tributory rivers are almost entirely contained within the continental United States. The magnitude of this river system is well stated by Mark Twain:

> The Mississippi . . . is in all ways remarkable. Consid-   *intranational*
> ering the Missouri its main branch, it is the longest river in
> the world—four thousand three hundred miles. . . . It dis-
> charges three times as much water as the St. Lawrence, twenty-
> five times as much as the Rhine. . . . No other river has so
> vast a drainage-basin: it draws its water supply from twenty-
> eight States and Territories; from Delaware on the Atlantic
> seaboard, and from all the country between that and Idaho
> on the Pacific slope—a spread of forty-five degrees of lon-
> gitude. The Mississippi receives and carries to the Gulf water
> from fifty-four subordinate rivers that are navigable by
> steamboats, and from some hundreds that are navigable by
> flats and keels. The area of its drainage-basin is as great as
> the combined areas of England, Wales, Scotland, Ireland,
> France, Spain, Portugal, Germany, Austria, Italy, and Turkey;
> and almost all this wide region is fertile; the Mississippi Val-
> ley, proper, is exceptionally so. (Twain, 1962)

Any program of unified flood control for as vast an inter-   *interstate*
state spatial region as the Mississippi drainage basin requires

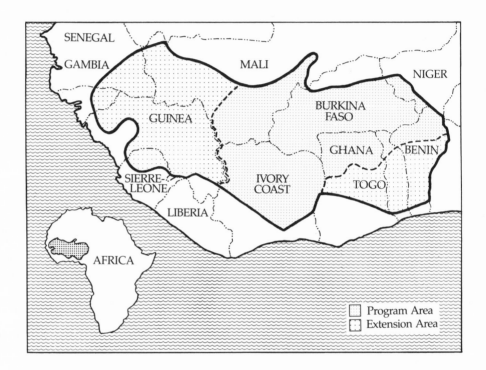

Figure 22
ONCHOCERCIASIS (RIVER BLINDNESS) CONTROL PROGRAM
International
Medicine
Operational
Reference: *Science*, 23 May 1986, p. 923.

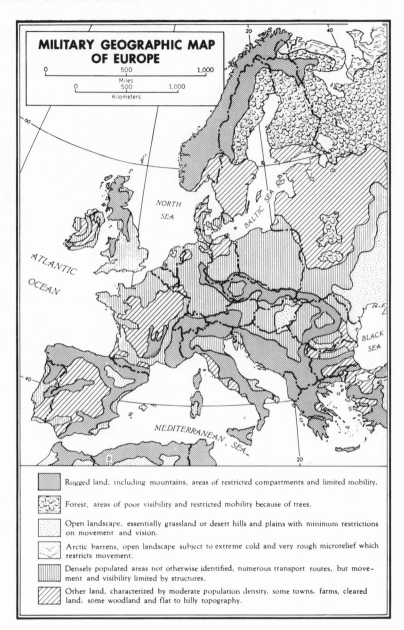

MILITARY GEOGRAPHIC MAP OF EUROPE

Rugged land, including mountains, areas of restricted compartments and limited mobility.

Forest, areas of poor visibility and restricted mobility because of trees.

Open landscape, essentially grassland or desert hills and plains with minimum restrictions on movement and vision.

Arctic barrens, open landscape subject to extreme cold and very rough microrelief which restricts movement.

Densely populated areas not otherwise identified, numerous transport routes, but movement and visibility limited by structures.

Other land, characterized by moderate population density, some towns, farms, cleared land, some woodland and flat to hilly topography.

Figure 23
MILITARY GEOGRAPHIC REGIONS
Geographic
Reference: Peltier, Louis C., and G. Etzel Pearcy, *Military Geography*,
New York (Van Nostrand), 1966, p. 87. Reprinted by permission
Wadsworth, Inc. ©

integrated policies and action programs by more than one-half
of the continental States (Figure 24, Major Drainage Basins,
page 50). On the other hand, the drought area in the southeastern United States shown in Figure 14 on page 31 is a small
interstate region, which is also temporary since it retains its
descriptive accuracy momentarily. The habitat of the black-footed
ferret is a region unique to this species threatened with extinction: composed of parts of 11 states and a small area in Canada
(Figure 25, Approximate Habitat: Black-Footed Ferret, page 51).
And the multi-purpose planning regions relating to the Tennessee Valley Authority have all been interstate. The original
region covering the drainage basin of the Tennessee River and
its tributaries, and its subsequent extension, are portrayed in

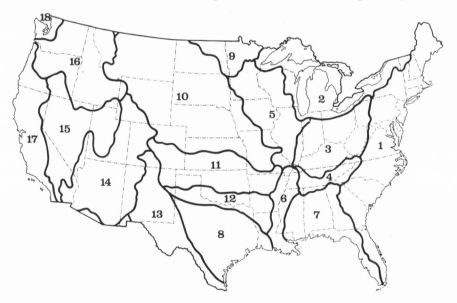

1-ATLANTIC   2-GREAT LAKES   3-OHIO   4-TENNESSEE   5-UPPER MISSISSIPPI
6-LOWER MISSISSIPPI   7-EASTERN GULF   8-WESTERN GULF   9-RED RIVER OF
THE NORTH   10-MISSOURI   11-ARKANSAS-WHITE   12-RED-QUACHITA   13-RIO
GRANDE   14-COLORADO   15-GREAT BASIN   16-COLUMBIA-SNAKE   17-SOUTH
PACIFIC   18-NORTH PACIFIC

Figure 24
MAJOR DRAINAGE BASINS
Intranational, InterState
Geography, Engineering
Descriptive
Reference: National Resources Committee, *Regional Factors in National
Planning*, Washington, DC (Government Printing Office), December 1935,
p. 171B.

Figure 26a on page 52. The surrounding area to which electricity was distributed is shown in Figure 26b, page 53.

A significant withdrawal of federal support and funding for such efforts [as the Tennessee Valley Authority has] occurred. . . . At the multi-state level, the federal-state regional commissions for river basin planning and economic development were abolished in 1981, though this development had only a very indirect impact on most localities. At the same time and unlike the administration, Congress did not sanction a full-scale retreat from the substate regional scene. Regional requirements still apply in such program areas as urban transportation, the aged, environmental protection, etc. Moreover, even [Executive Order] 12372 provides for a back-up federal role, though clearly the states are left to serve as the key actors in the enduring substate regional drama. (Walker, 1986)

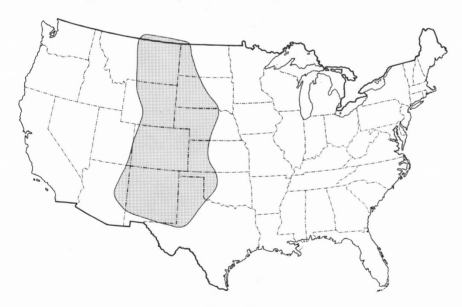

Figure 25
APPROXIMATE HABITAT: BLACK-FOOTED FERRET
Intracontinental, Interstate
Zoology
Research
Reference: Crowe, Douglas M., *Furbearers of Wyoming*, Cheyenne, WY (Wyoming Game and Fish Department), 1986. Courtesy of Larry L. Kruckenberg, Game and Fish Department, State of Wyoming.

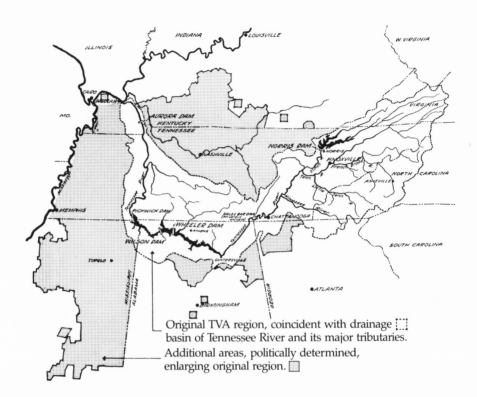

Original TVA region, coincident with drainage
basin of Tennessee River and its major tributaries.
Additional areas, politically determined,
enlarging original region.

Figure 26a
TENNESSEE VALLEY AUTHORITY: JURISDICTION
Interstate
Engineering, Civil Government
Economic Development
References: National Resources Committee, *Regional Factors in National
Planning*, Washington, DC (Government Printing Office), 1935, p. 84.
Tennessee Valley Authority, *A Student History of the TVA*, Knoxville, TN
(Information Office), TVA/OGM/10–84/85, p. 18.

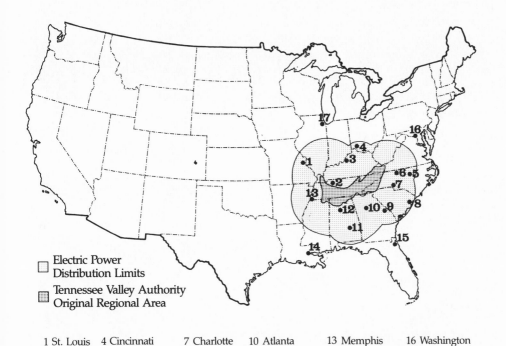

Electric Power
Distribution Limits

Tennessee Valley Authority
Original Regional Area

1 St. Louis   4 Cincinnati   7 Charlotte   10 Atlanta   13 Memphis   16 Washington
2 Nashville   5 Raleigh   8 Charleston   11 Montgomery 14 New Orleans 17 Chicago
3 Louisville 6 Winston Salem 9 Augusta   12 Birmingham 15 Jacksonville

Figure 26b
TENNESSEE VALLEY AUTHORITY: INITIAL POWER DISTRIBUTION
Interstate
Engineering, Civil Government
Operational
Reference: National Resources Committee, *Regional Factors in National
Planning*, Washington, DC (Government Printing Office), December 1935,
p. 112.

The regional concept is as useful for states as it is for other applications. Its descriptive value is illustrated clearly by California with its geographical and geological diversity: deserts, mountain chains with high-altitude alpine meadows, a long coastline, large inland valleys, areas with geothermal springs and strong prevailing winds. Each of these constitutes an intrastate region sufficiently unique to require particular treatment or permitting special use. Producing electricity by wind-driven generators is an example, since they can be located only in certain places with the necessary microclimatic conditions. Figure 27 on page 55 depicts three intrastate regions relating to wind resources in California. The shaded areas are parts of a discontinuous region where wind measuring instruments determine whether wind driven generators can produce electrical energy at feasible cost. A second set of discontinuous areas, much smaller in size, is where "wind farms" and two large utility-owned wind-driven electric generators have been built. And the directional arrows extending throughout the state indicate generally the regions where prevailing winds occur. They are irregular, discontinuous, fluctuating, and indefinitely bounded.

Politics limit the operational use of intrastate regions. Although local governments are "creatures of the state," municipalities and counties resist any reduction in "home rule" or transfer of local decision making to a higher level of government. Nonetheless, regional arrangements are being made when local governments cannot cope with problems or needs that extend beyond their spatial boundaries or financial resources. Implementation of the Federal Coastal Management Act illustrates the need for state involvement in the use of land in the geographically special and economically important coastline areas. It also illustrates the extent to which this involvement is limited by the resistance of counties and municipalities to any permanent reduction in local authority.

intrastate   Intrastate regions are established because crucial needs and critical problems extend across local governmental boundaries. Air pollution control districts must include the counties and municipalities contained within the geographical airshed. Few flood control watersheds are contained within a single county.

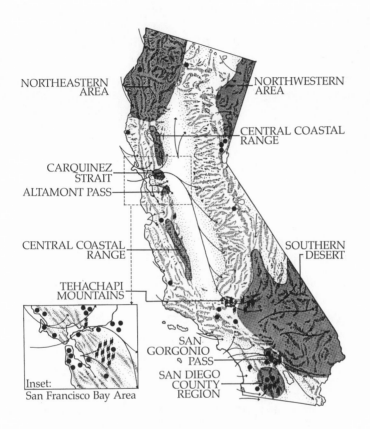

NORTHEASTERN AREA

NORTHWESTERN AREA

CENTRAL COASTAL RANGE

CARQUINEZ STRAIT

ALTAMONT PASS

CENTRAL COASTAL RANGE

SOUTHERN DESERT

TEHACHAPI MOUNTAINS

SAN GORGONIO PASS

SAN DIEGO COUNTY REGION

Inset:
San Francisco Bay Area

☐ Resource Assessment Areas   → Prevailing Wind Directions
        ●Anemometer Loan Projects (Wind Speed Measurement)
⚡Wind Farms   ⚡Large, Utility-Owned Wind Turbines

Figure 27
WIND RESOURCES: CALIFORNIA
Intrastate
Geography, Engineering
Descriptive
Discontinuous, Fluctuating, Indefinite
Reference: California Energy Commission, *California Wind Atlas*,
Sacramento, CA (California Department of Water Resources), April 1985,
p. 10, cover.

intercounty   Most intercounty regions, or districts as they are more commonly called, are established to provide a single utility or other
public service which individual counties cannot provide for
themselves because of geographical conditions or insufficient
resources. A metropolitan regional water district, organized to
import water which no local government can provide by itself,
illustrates the first of these situations. And because most local
governments do not have the financial resources to meet their
own public health needs, they contract with a larger governmental unit or combine in an intercounty operational region to
provide the needed services. The number of intercounty regions
depends in part on the size of the counties, which range from
20,102 square miles in San Bernardino County, California, to
22 square miles in New York County, New York.

         From 1957 through 1977, the number of special purpose
    districts, which provide such services as water, sewage,
    transportation and drainage, increased from 14,424 to
    26,140. These districts usually have taxing power and gov-
    erning bodies separate from their cities and counties. Cit-
    izens under their jurisdiction rarely know how they oper-
    ate, yet they have become an important part of the Federal
    System. (*The New York Times*, 12 November 1978)

metropolitan   Metropolitan regional planning—discussed and illustrated
beginning on pages 101 and 191—requires coordinating the
activities of the separate independent municipalities that are
incorporated within the urbanized area as it expands into the
countryside surrounding the original community. In addition
to the county containing the principal city, metropolitan statistical areas as defined by the U.S. Census include other counties
having strong economic and social ties to the central county.
Most metropolitan regions include several counties. Metropolitan regional planning becomes increasingly important as
the size of these conurbations and the number of local governments within them increase.

intracounty   The smallest operating regions are those contained within
municipal   counties or municipalities of average size. Like intercounty
regions, most of them are created to provide particular public
services. Small descriptive regions are employed at the local

level: for example, to identify geological conditions requiring stronger and more costly construction to maintain minimum building standards, or more restrictive zoning limiting the use of land or the height of buildings in these areas. Also, regions within the county or city may be delineated where steep slopes restrict emergency access and substantially increase the costs of installing and maintaining public utilities and services; usually the densities of development permitted in such areas are less than in flat and moderately sloped sections of the municipality or county (Figure 28, Mountain Fire Districts and Hillside Areas, page 58).

In this chapter space limitations have required the selection of single or several examples to illustrate different kinds of regions. No attempt is made to cover every particular or unique kind of region. There are many examples of the use of each type of region by the three major classifications of their application: civil government, business, and the military services. Almost every region selected illustrates some characteristic of another kind of region, with respect to boundaries, spatial extent, form, contiguity, flexibility, definiteness, permanence, or some other attribute. Almost every region exemplifies several aspects of its type. Normally, they serve several purposes.

REFERENCES

[1] Canby, Thomas Y., "El Niño's Ill Winds," *National Geographic*, February 1984, p. 181. [2] Christol, Carl Q., "Space Law: Justice for the New Frontier," *Sky & Telescope*, November 1984, p. 408. [3] Clines, Francis X., "British Planning to Curb Acid Rain," *The New York Times*, 12 September 1986, p. Y5. [4] Coniff, Richard, "Inventorying life in the 'biotic frontier' before it disappears," *Smithsonian*, September 1986, p. 81. [5] Dickson, David, "Europe Struggles to Control Pollution," *Science*, 12 December 1986, p. 1315. [6] Gore, Rick, "An Age-Old Challenge Grows," *National Geographic*, November 1979, pp. 604–606. [7] Keller, Edward J., *Environmental Geology*, Second Edition, Columbus, OH (Merrill), 1979, p. 303. [8] Kronholz, June, "Mysterious Monsoons Dictate Fate of India And Its Farm Output," *The Wall Street Journal*, 26 August 1986, p. 1. [9] Maris, Michael A., "Conservation in South America: Problems, Consequences, and Solutions," *Science*, 15 August 1986, pp. 735, 738. [10] Margulis, Lynn, and Dorian Sagan, *Microcosmos*, Four Billion Years of Evolution From Our Microbial Ancestors, New York (Summit), 1986, pp. 45, 46. [11] Marshall, Eliot, "Space Junk Grows with Weapons Tests," *Science*, 25 October 1985, p. 424. [12] Mumford, Lewis, *The Culture*

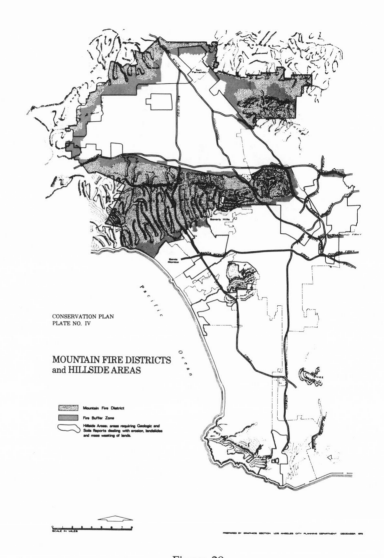

CONSERVATION PLAN
PLATE NO. IV

MOUNTAIN FIRE DISTRICTS
and HILLSIDE AREAS

Mountain Fire District

Fire Buffer Zone

Hillside Areas: areas requiring Geologic and
Soils Reports dealing with erosion, landslides
and mass wasting of lands.

Figure 28
MOUNTAIN FIRE DISTRICTS AND HILLSIDE AREAS
Metropolitan
Geography
Planning, Operations
Reference: City Planning Department, *Conservation Plan*, Los Angeles, CA
(Graphics Section), December 1973.

of Cities, New York (Harcourt, Brace), 1938, p. 301. [13] Museum of Natural History, Exhibit: *Late Ice-Age Art*, New York, NY, December, 1986. [14] National Archives of the United States, *United States Directory of Federal Regional Structure, 1981/82*, Washington, DC (Government Printing Office), 1982, p. 11. [15] *The New York Times*, 12 November 1978, p. 74. [16] *The New York Times*, 23 July 1985, p. Y2. [17] *The New York Times*, 9 September 1986, p. 22Y. [18] "Nuclear Debris in Space Seen Danger to Earth," *The New York Times*, 23 September 1986, p. Y25. [19] Patterson, Bruce D., "Species Loss," *Science*, Letters, 12 December 1986, p. 1311. [20] Riding, Alan, "In Brazil, Environmentalists Enjoy a Rare Taste of Success," *The New York Times*, 23 July 1985, p. Y20. [21] Saarinen, Thomas F., *Environmental Planning*, Perception and Behavior, Boston (Houghton Mifflin), 1976, pp. 185, 187. [22] Shabecoff, Philip, "Swifter Warming of the Globe Foreseen," *The New York Times*, 6 November 1986, p. Y1. [23] Sheffield, Charles, *Men on Earth*, How Civilization and Technology Changed the Face of the World—A Survey from Space, New York (Macmillan), 1983, p. 20. [24] Sun, Marjorie, "Ground Water Ills: Many Diagnoses, Four Remedies," *Science*, 20 June 1986, p. 1490. [25] Twain, Mark, *Life on the Mississippi*, New York (Oxford University Press), 1962, p. 1. [26] Waldrop, M. Mitchell, "Astronomers Find Their First Embryonic Star," *Science*, 22 August 1986, p. 841. [27] _____"Sighting of a Supernova," *Science*, 6 March 1987, p. 1143. [28] Walker, David B., "Intergovernmental Relations and the Well-Groomed City: Cooperation, Confrontation, Clarification," *National Civic Review*, March-April 1986, p. 80.

So far, economists, geographers, physical planners and sociologists have recognized the specific character of regional development as well as the need to explain the phenomenon, but neither of these scientists has been successful in presenting a doctrine. Nevertheless, the necessity for such a doctrine is being experienced more and more now that many governments in the developed and developing parts of the world have decided to embark upon or to continue with regional planning efforts.

Development Centre, Organization for Economic Co-Operation and Development, *Multidisciplinary Aspects of Regional Development*, 1969.

CHAPTER 2
ACADEMIC USES OF REGIONS

ALMOST ALL of the regions noted in the previous chapter were identified initially by an academic discipline or field of study for its own purposes. Every intellectual endeavor makes use of or relates to the regional concept in some way. As each discipline extends the depth and breadth of its knowledge, its employment of the regional concept in education, research, planning, and operations progresses accordingly. Examples of this utilization or relationship are given for a number of fields in this chapter. Several of these that are sparsely treated in the literature relating to regions are illustrated at greater length here. It is neither feasible nor necessary to cover all disciplines and fields to indicate the universality and importance of the regional concept.

Around the world regions suitable for different crops and types of farming have been identified. Besides the locational effects of climate, soils, drainage, seed selection, and farm practices: *agricultural science*

> The dominance of a certain crop in a certain region comes about as a result of the integration of a number of economic ecological factors. The dominant crop is well adapted to the environment and gives a high yield. It also fits well into the plan of farm management and has a relatively low risk of failure. A market is available that makes it possible for the crop to serve as the basis for a good income to the farmer. (Loomis, 1976)

Agricultural regions of the United States—such as the midwestern corn and wheat belts, California and Florida citrus areas, locations suitable for vineyards in the eastern and western United States—are well known. Rice growing areas in Asia were identified thousands of years ago.

Only about 3.2 billion hectares [2.471 billion acres] of the total 13 billion hectares of the earth's ice-free land surface can be cultivated. . . .

The highest concentrations of arable land lie in the semiarid, subhumid, and humid grasslands of the middle latitudes. . . .

Besides arable lands, an additional 3.6 billion hectares of the earth's surface could serve for grazing livestock. . . .

Because their climates allow growing two or more crops a year over vast regions, the largest potential cropped areas are in the developing countries of Asia, Africa, and Latin America. . . . (Revelle, 1976)

Some crops require very special geographic, climatic, and micro-meterological environments. For example, even within the few areas in California favorable for the commercial growing of avocados shown in Figure 29 on page 63 there may be limitations ". . . of land elevation, wind currents and other factors. These may occur within short distances, one to another, and even within the same ranch or portion of a property. A curious state, and a curious fruit" (Borton, 1986).

Both subsistence and commercial farming require particular agronomic conditions. Subsistence farming is more dispersed regionally because it is smaller in size, simpler if not rudimentary, and performed by individual families or small groups of related people. In many parts of the world there is a tradition or governmental policy favoring subsistence farming.

Commercial farms, producing products of sufficient quality to be sold to the public, are mechanized, require much larger areas of level land, modern agricultural practices and equipment, and a considerable financial investment. They are usually concentrated in smaller regions providing the necessary environmental conditions.

anthropology   As the study of the relation of environment, race, and culture to the evolution of human beings and the development of civilization, anthropology is probably concerned with as many different regions as any field of study. This is evident in the dictionary definition of the field as:

Figure 29

. . . the science of man in relation to his physical character (anthropography, anthropometry), to his historical and geographical distribution (anthropogeography, ethnography), to the origin, classification, and relationship of races (ethnology), to his environmental and social relations (anthroponomy, demography, sociology), and to the history of culture (prehistoric anthropology, human paleontology, archaeology, folklore, and religions). (*Webster's New International Dictionary of the English Language*, 1960)

AVOCADOS: COMMERCIAL PRODUCTION
Intrastate
Geography, Agricultural Science
Discontinuous
Reference: Borton, Dean E. (Director of Communications, Calavo Growers of California, Los Angeles, CA), Written Communication, 3 November 1986.

Regions are involved in each of the subdivisions of anthropology. For example, differences in the physical characteristics of man in different parts of the world are immediately apparent. The social relations between people living in artic regions, deserts, or metropolises have developed differently because of the great differences in the physical environments. Within these expanses the academic specialist distinguishes subregions displaying subtle but significant social and cultural differences. The historical and geographical distribution of humans throughout history has involved regions of earliest origin such as east Africa and Australia, and regional pathways of prehistorical movement between continents such as the land bridges which existed long ago between Africa and Europe, and between Asia and North America.

Archeologists and anthropologists are discerning a major, previously unrecognized phase in the development of early civilization. . . . complex, sophisticated economic and social systems developed 7,000–9,000 years ago— 1,000–3,000 years before the first cities rose and humans began to write things down. . . . The new image . . . suggests that those factors considered so important in the formation of cities and states actually were elements in a stable form much earlier. . . . The huge village, really a town, called Catal Huyuk in south-central Turkey . . . may therefore be the Pompei of the era and the region. (Stevens, 1986)

Human culture has always reflected the physical environment: directly in the local materials used for art objects; and indirectly by the progressive interrelation between the regional environment, the culture it shapes, and the content and form of artistic expression.

The symbols found on Upper Paleolithic cave walls show both similarity and differences through time and space . . . four stylistic stages in the evolution of Upper Paleolithic art, each with its own set of symbols and conventions, which varied according to region (Museum of Natural History, 1986).

architecture   The global and regional distribution of different religions is a cultural force that affects many anthropological studies in some way (Figure 30, Major World Religions, page 65).

From earliest times, dwellings have related to their geographical surroundings. Construction materials and methods of providing the basic requirements of shelter—protection from rain, temperature extremes, and high winds—differ among polar, temperate, tropical, desert, and other environmentally distinct regions. For example, high-pitched roofs are more common in regions with heavy snowfall. Walls are generally thicker, overhangs deeper, and arcades more widely employed in arctic and tropical regions with extreme temperatures.

Geological ground conditions determine the foundations required to support different structures. In the United States, structural requirements also vary among the regions of seismic risk designated in local building codes, illustrated in Figure 31, Seismic Risk, page 66. The desires, customs, and habits of people in a particular area are apparent in the design of their buildings. We observe almost daily in periodicals or on television the differences between the residential, civic, and religious architecture of primitive and industrial societies, culturally distinct regions, or those with long established stylistic heritages. There are also forces promoting architectural uniformity: the cost advantages of steel-frame construction for highrise office buildings, or the common features desired in dwelling units engendered by worldwide television.

Besides those noted previously on page 38 as examples of global regions, there are references throughout the *Larousse Encyclopedia of Astronomy* to general and specific astronomical regions: for example, certain B-type stars "are strongly clustered about the galactic equator, and . . . are especially numerous in the region of Perseus and Sagittarius (and probably beyond, in the more southerly region of the Milky Way from

astronomy

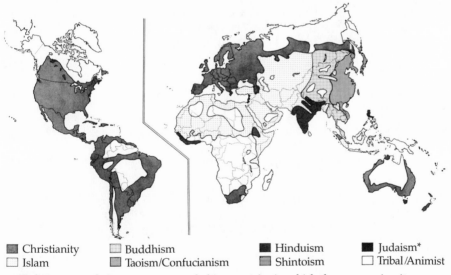

| ■ Christianity | ▦ Buddhism | ■ Hinduism | ■ Judaism* |
| □ Islam | ▦ Taoism/Confucianism | ▤ Shintoism | □ Tribal/Animist |

*Religious populations are not recorded in countries in which they are a minority.

Figure 30
MAJOR WORLD RELIGIONS
Global
Sociology
Descriptive
Reference: Gaisford, John (Editor), *Atlas of Man*, New York (St. Martin's),
1978, p. 21.

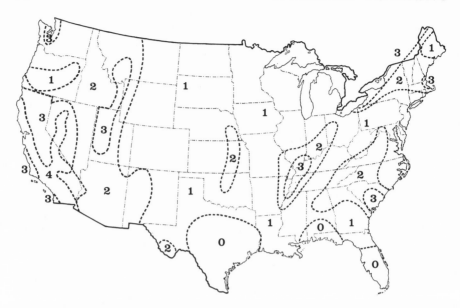

ZONE 0 - No damage.   ZONE 1 - Minor damage; distant earthquakes may cause damage to struc-
tures with fundamental periods greater than 1.0 second ; corresponds to intensities V and VI of the
Modified Mercalli Intensity Scale (M.M.).   ZONE 2 - Moderate damage; corresponds to intensity
VII of the M.M. Scale.   ZONE 3 - Major damage; corresponds to intensity VII and higher of the
M.M. Scale.   ZONE 4 - Those areas within Zone No. 3 determined by the proximity to certain
major fault systems.

Figure 31
SEISMIC RISK
Intranational
Geology, Engineering
Descriptive
Reference: International Conference of Building Officials, *Uniform Building
Code*, 1985 Edition, Whittier, CA, 1 May 1985, p. 135.

Centaurus to Argo . . .)"; or "the law of stellar reddening also
appears to vary from one region to another. . . ." (Rudaux,
1959). Most of the spatial designations in astronomy are nodal
in nature referring to galaxies, nebulae, stars, and other astronomical entities. Although the term region is used infrequently
compared to this identification of spaces with reference to specific celestial bodies, these spaces are nodal regions as defined
in this book.

biology   From the end of the 15th century the western nations
of Europe were sending forth expeditions east and west,
and these brought home knowledge of the natural prod-

ucts of lands newly explored. Thus the idea that each region has its characteristic living things, implicit in ancient biology but forgotten during the middle ages, became gradually explicit. . . . Quite apart from the investigations and theories with which Darwin's name is especially associated, the voyage [of HMS Beagle] was important in making accessible a whole multitude of new forms of zoo-geographical and phyto-geographical regions. (*The Encyclopaedia Britannica*, 1929)

Recent advances made possible by the electron microscope, remote sensing, and high altitude research vehicles have extended biological knowledge in both microscopic and macroscopic directions.

Greater understanding has been developed concerning the structure and behavior of the infinitesimally small: bacteria, fungi, algae, cells, viruses, and the genetic code which controls the development of all animate organisms. The regions considered in this book do not apply at this small scale.

In the macroscopic direction much has been learned concerning the earth's biosphere: the terrestrial space or spherical region enveloping the earth within about 10,000 meters above and below ground level, in which liquid water exists in substantial quantities, external energy is received from the sun, and there are interfaces between liquid, solid, and gaseous states of matter. All living things depend on this environmental region subject to gradual change by natural evolutionary forces operating within the biosphere.

This critical region is also subject to rapid and significant change brought about by human activities affecting the earth's surface waters and underground aquifers, ground surface and underground, and encompassing atmosphere. These activities impact the environment separately, and in various combinations may contaminate the atmosphere, pollute surface and underground waters, or threaten natural habitats by an excessive intrusion of people.

As a branch of biology, botany is a basic constituent of the *botany* biosphere. In dictionary terminology botany is regional in nature involving "plant life, as of a region, as the botany of Labrador." Plants contribute some 60 percent of the oxygen in the earth's atmosphere; they are the primary determinant of the agricultural regions of the world, and the principal element of tropical rain forests. Plants interrelate in some way with every aspect of the physical and animal worlds. They provide food, the only water for some animals, clothing, shelter, construction and manufacturing materials, medicines, psychological sustenance, and visual pleasure. Each characteristic and use of plants relates to an area or region where the botanical organism can exist, grow, and propagate. The world is filled with a multitude of such botanical regions. Plants are rooted literally and figuratively in related physical space.

business management   Regions are relevant to business in many ways, but they are mainly employed in connection with production, distribution, marketing, sales, strategic and operational management. Consumer oriented enterprises relate their advertising and sales efforts to the purchasing power of different sections of the country, as shown in Figure 37, Buying Power, page 77. Climatic and geographical differences affect the demand for many products. Most advertising, marketing, and the production they generate are related to regional differences in age groups, educational level, median income, religious affiliation, and other characteristics that affect customer demand, product and service preferences, personal habits and attitudes, and behavioral patterns. Specifically, color choice, taste preference, or the exact product type desired may vary significantly among regions. (Figure 32, Consumer Products Markets, page 69)

> In the next ten years, the population of the nine-state . . . region will increase by more than 6.5 million . . . 44% faster than the national rate, so that by the year 2000, more than 56 million people will be living in the Southeast.
>
> More people mean more new homes and more new jobs: over 4.5 million new housing starts and more than 4 million new jobs. In fact, the region's employment figure will grow at a rate 40% faster than the national rate. Real personal income will rise by 3.0% per year as compared with 2.8% for the nation. (Bell South, 1986)

Regions also relate to operational management. Many large organizations have found that attempting to direct all activities

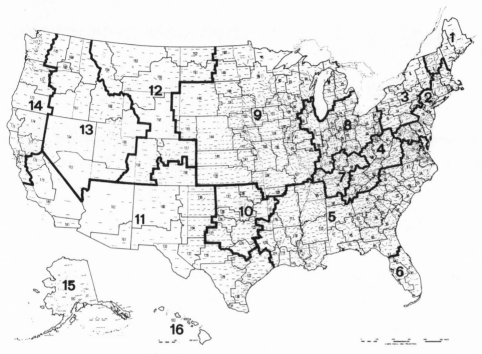

Regions: 1. Yankee Belt 2. Boston-Washington 3. Eastern Foundry 4. Southern Appalachia 5. Dixie 6. South Florida 7. Mid South 8. Western Foundry 9. Midwest Great Plains 10. Plains Energy 11. Hispanic America 12. Western Energy Belt 13. The Empty Corridor 14. Pacific Northwest 15. Alaska 16. Hawaiian Islands.

Figure 32
CONSUMER PRODUCTS MARKETS
Intranational
Business Management, Economics
Descriptive
Reference: Rubel, Thomas I., *Geographical Patterns of Growth*, Dublin, OH
(Management Horizons), 1982, p. 7.

from a single headquarters is not successful or is less efficient than decentralized management. Accordingly, regional spaces and regional positions are established (Figure 33, Nationally Advertised Regional Positions in Business, page 70). They may be concerned with a single function such as advertising, sales, product distribution, manufacturing, or servicing (Figure 34, Automotive Manufacture: Sales, page 71). Or regional executives may be responsible for all activities within their jurisdiction, subject to policies determined centrally, limitations on capital spending, and profitable operations.

REGIONAL:
Bio-Geographer
Business Development
Clinical Associates
Controller
Credit Supervisor
Director:
  Insurance Sales
  Labor Relations
  Marketing
  Operations
  Planning
  Security
  Strategic Planning
Ecologist:
  Aquatic
  Watershed
Finance Officer
Manager:
  Audit
  Automotive Specialist
  Business
  Construction
  Consumer Products
  Credit
  Dealers, Rep Organizations

Educational Services
Loans
Marketing
Mortgage Banking
Office
Personnel
Planning and Finance
Process Control
Projects
Properties
Public Affairs
Retail Banking
Sales
Sales Engineers
Sales and Service
Senior Vice President and Regional
  Director
Vice President:
  Audit Management
  Commercial Lending
  Mortgage Loan Centers
  Office
  Property
  Real Estate Investment
  Sales

Figure 33

NATIONALLY ADVERTISED REGIONAL POSITIONS IN BUSINESS*

*Positions advertised in *The New York Times* (National Edition), *The Wall Street Journal*, *Los Angeles Times*, and *Science* Magazine during a period of approximately six months during 1985–1986.

Figure 34
AUTOMOTIVE MANUFACTURE: SALES
Intranational
Business Management
Operational
Reference: Market Research Manager, Personal Communication, 22
September 1986.

As business and industry become national and international in scope, new or expanded regional considerations emerge. Regional banking is a recent development.

> A clear signal of change flashed . . . when the United States Supreme Court upheld the constitutionality of regional interstate banking laws. Under these reciprocal pacts, two or more states establish regions in which member banks may merge across state lines, while banks from outside the region are not admitted. These mergers are speeding the development of super-regional banks. (Vartan, 1985)

Market analysis usually determines in which areas of the world present sales efforts should be intensified or new sales regions established. For example, 20 years ago an aircraft manufacturer identified Core Areas of the World where commitments to buy commercial airplanes were most likely to be made in 1985 (Figure 35, page 73).

> This report incorporates the initial results of an extensive survey of environmental factors which may influence the . . . industry over the next 20 years. The report is still preliminary pending completion of a Technical Environment Analysis.
>
> A composite 20-year forecast, a matrix summary of time-phased elements of each environmental consideration, will be prepared on completion of the Technical Environment section. (Quick, 1966)

ecology   As defined, ecology "deals with the mutual relationship among organisms and between them and their environments." This signifies a regional relationship since the biology of organisms interrelates with the characteristics of their habitat. The Serengeti in east Africa, extending from southern Kenya to northern Tanzania, is a regional ecosystem more familiar than most such systems because of frequent references to it in scientific journals, news media, and television programs (Figure 36, Serengeti, page 74). It is an outstanding example of the extraordinary subtleties of ecosystems, which in this case can extend across national borders.

CORE AREAS IN THE WORLD
1985

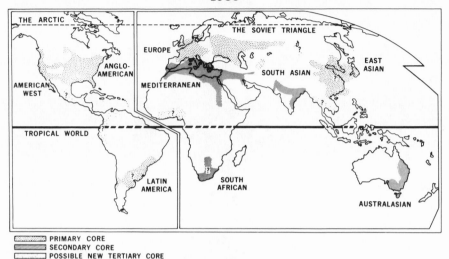

PRIMARY CORE
SECONDARY CORE
POSSIBLE NEW TERTIARY CORE

Figure 35
CORE AREAS IN THE WORLD
Global, Intercontinental, Intracontinental
Economics, Political Science
Planning
Reference: Quick, L.H., *Planning Report*, Operation Spade, The Future
World Environment, A Twenty-Year Forecast, Douglas Air Group, Long
Beach, CA, 22 March 1966, p. 125.

In the Serengeti, predation maintains a balance between the population of different animal species and the habitat each requires for survival. At the same time, animal behavior adjusts to counter any serious threats to survival. Sedentary species exist within the spatial territories they establish and defend for themselves. Migratory animals follow the grasslands as the forage is renewed by seasonal rains. The interrelationships between flora and fauna in the grassslands of the Serengeti illustrate the subtlety of this ecosystem. One after the other, each of several species of antelope crops a portion of the grass stalk until it is eaten so close to the ground it no longer provides sustenance. After frequent fires, seasonal rains, and regrowth of the grass, the cycle is repeated.

What had by now become apparent was . . . [that] the grasslands of Serengeti formed a self-sustaining ecological

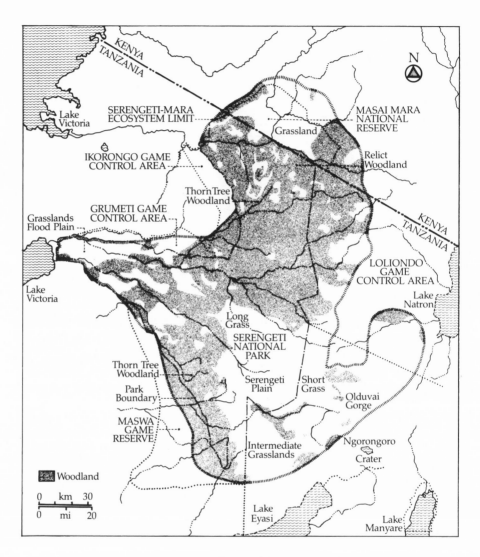

Figure 36
SERENGETI
International
Ecology
Descriptive
Reference: Alexander, Shana,"The Serengeti, The Glory of Life," *National Geographic*, May 1986, p. 589.

system, a vast and unique complex of higher mammalian life interacting responsively with its environment. Everything was interdependent—fire, rain, soil, grass, and a host of animals. Each living thing depended on the other, each flourished because of the other. Serengeti, with its extraordinary residents—from tiny, nearly blind mole rats to majestic giraffes, was proceeding, still comparatively undisturbed, through an evolutionary process that has been going on for hundreds of thousands of years.

Serengeti remains the great anachronism, its survival maintained through an odd, near-mystical series of countervailing conditions, which have thus far managed to tip a fragile balance slightly to the side of the animals: drought and famine versus population increases; pestilence and disease versus cattle proliferation; tourist income versus pressure for land cultivation; the vagaries of nature versus scientific research. (Hayes, 1976)

The ecological approach to land classification and utilization has now won general acceptance, but its value is accentuated in Kenya by the wide range of conditions that occur—from glacial peaks to semi-desert—and by the current demands of a growing human population, occurring at a time of accelerated economic development.

The factors determining the inherent potential of a unit of land are its climate, topography, and soil. The basic ecological land unit—the working basis for detailed planning and management—is therefore a unit of land which is differentiated by reference to each of these three factors. (Pratt, 1970)

The creation, use, distribution, and effects of wealth relate *economics* to regions. Agricultural, industrial, commercial, and other productive enterprises require certain resources and conditions available only in certain places. These may involve soils, climate, weather, raw materials, labor supply, customers, transportation facilities, financial support, or any one of many geographical, demographic, or institutional requirements.

Reduced taxes, financial incentives, employee training, and other inducements provided by a state or local government seeking to bolster its economy may persuade a productive activity to locate within its area rather than where location economics indicate. The developmnt of economically depressed regions such as Appalachia in the United States and southwestern France, discussed in Chapter 4, requires strengthening existing enterprises and attracting new productive endeavors. Most nations believe that they benefit socially and culturally when no section of the country is economically depressed compared with other regions.

The economies of metropolitan regions represent their productive capability and determine their general condition. These urban areas are vital to the economic health of nations with large percentages of their population and productive activities located in these centers. Metropolitan urban regions in the United States now house 75 percent of the population. They will soon contain 50 percent of the people of the world.

Most enterprises must consider regional conditions. The purchasing power of different sections of the country is taken into account in organizing their product advertising, sales, and distribution (Figure 37, Buying Power, page 77). Inventory storage is placed with reference to regional demand for the product and its transportation cost. Economic considerations are involved in the initial decision by many organizations to decentralize operations in selecting the size and shape of the operating regions and locating field offices.

Characteristic or unexpected regional events can have far-reaching consequences. The economic significance of the monsoon for several continents and of seismic risk in certain regions is noted on pages 43 and 66. Regions subject to periodic flooding, destructive weather, or other environmental hazards are economically vulnerable.

engineering   Even more directly than economics, engineering—"the art and science by which the properties of matter and the sources of power in nature are made useful to man in structures, machines, and manufactured products" —relates to regions of almost all kinds. Building codes are more stringent in areas of greater seismic risk because of the additional engineering requirements imposed by local governments to ensure structural safety. Climate affects the need for insulation, air conditioning, provision for snow and wind loads, and the expansion

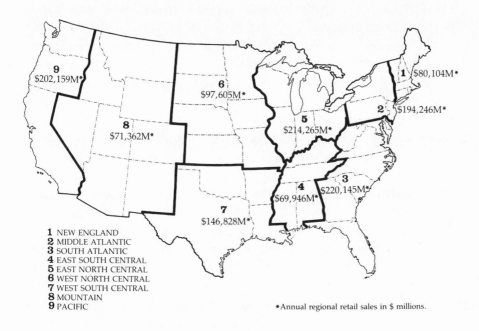

1 NEW ENGLAND
2 MIDDLE ATLANTIC
3 SOUTH ATLANTIC
4 EAST SOUTH CENTRAL
5 EAST NORTH CENTRAL
6 WEST NORTH CENTRAL
7 WEST SOUTH CENTRAL
8 MOUNTAIN
9 PACIFIC   *Annual regional retail sales in $ millions.

Figure 37
BUYING POWER
Intranational
Business, Economics
Research
Reference: *S & MM*, 1985 Survey of Buying Power, 22 July 1985, p. A-5.

and contraction of materials. Geological conditions determine foundation requirements and the design of underground utilities without which communities in the industrialized countries could not function. The accessibility and use of natural resources depend on engineering: coal, iron ore, and precious metal deposits, oil and gas fields, aquifers, and sources of potential water power. These resources and physical conditions requiring engineering often occur in space as regions, or are associated with a geographical or geological region.

Engineering can, of course, also create regions. For example, when an extensive system of water wells and irrigation produces an agricultural complex within a desert area, as has been done in various parts of the world; or when unique engineering structures and methods were developed by The Netherlands over several centuries enabling large areas to be reclaimed from the sea, creating new regions for agriculture, housing, and other uses.

geography   Geography, or natural philosophy as it was called in ancient times, was probably the first of the academic disciplines to apply the regional concept extensively. As the field whose primary purpose is to study the physical world and its relation to humans, its spatial concerns range from areas of small size to global views encompassing the entire earth. Regions have a primary place in this spectrum of areal consideration because they depict real conditions as they exist or occur on the ground or in atmospheric space. These are the phenomena of greatest interest to geographers, usually conceived and presented in map form. They are not defined by jurisdictional boundaries except when political or governmental aspects are relevant. Most of the illustrations in this book selected as examples of various kinds or characteristics of regions depict geographical regions, such as those considered by the armed services in planning and carrying out any military operations in western Europe (Figure 23, Military Geographical Regions, page 49).

geology   Geology, originally part of geography, utilizes the regional concept in the same basic way as its parent field, except its focus is on the nature and disposition of the underground materials of the earth, its internal structure, and the dynamic forces that are continuously active within the terrestrial globe. The titles of a number of the figures on previous pages indicate that geological regions were involved in a variety of activities: Figure 3, Major Salt Deposits, page 14; Figure 15, Underground Water Resources, page 32; Figure 17, Major Lithosphere Plates, page 39; Figure 31, Seismic Risk, page 66; and Figure 38, Iodine Content of Drinking Water and Goiter Frequency, page 82. The Mountain Fire Districts and Hillside Areas shown in Figure 28 on page 58 indicate urban areas in which both geographic and geologic conditions justify restrictions on building density and the imposition of special requirements in construction.

Landscape architecture is concerned with open spaces *landscape* ranging from small intimate gardens to large parks, recrea- *architecture* tional areas, highway rights-of-way, and the vegetative treatment and land uses permitted along coastlines, in desert lands, and in other natural environments occupying hundreds or thousands of acres.

In all landscaping, regional characteristics and conditions are involved in the selection of vegetation to be planted or preserved. As a particular example, increased contamination of the air over most large cities in industrialized countries has necessitated selection of pollution resistant plants and trees for new installations, and replacement of existing vegetation over a period of years in many communities. In ruralities, regional considerations affect the size, disposition, and use of fields, timber stands, hedgerows, windbreaks, water bodies, and other physical features of the countryside. Ecological balance, mitigating and taking advantage of environmental impacts induced by man, are regional objectives.

All of these applications and considerations require a regional awareness to meet the requirements and opportunities presented by nature and the environmental effects of human activities. "Design with Nature" is a method of large-scale landscape planning to locate facilities significantly impacting the regional environment. Environmental protection legislation and environmental impact reporting in the United States are responsive to regional concerns and objectives.

The specialties of maritime, space, land planning, and envi- *law* ronmental law incorporate the regional concept in the established content of the law and in legal education. Each has to do with a region: the oceans of the world, inner and outer space above the earth, land areas ranging from small to very large, and the space at, above, and below ground level involved in the immediate human environment. In practice, law addresses more specific regional issues. It is deeply involved in regional water rights and related matters, environmental pollution, regional banking, regional planning, and the many other activities of man having to do with one or more of the numerous kinds of regions. Law is the primary force in the formulation of legislation involving regions, the litigation of subsequent disputes, and the resolution of appeals to the courts. For example, California state legislation provides that counties and municipalities that enact laws restricting the number of new housing units built within their jurisdictions each year

> shall consider the effect of ordinances adopted . . . on the housing needs of the region in which the local jurisdiction is situated and balance these needs against the public service needs of its residents and available fiscal and financial resources. (California Government Code: Section 65853.6)

To the extent legal education includes regional considerations in the substance of the curriculum, it is concerning itself with this broad subject as it is treated in this book.

In recent years a new relationship with regions has come about. Some law firms have grown so large that operational efficiency requires the establishment of regional offices managed by senior partners of the parent firm.

medicine   The relationships between medicine and regions are similar to those between law and geographical spaces. The connection between certain diseases of humans and other animals and particular places was noted early in human history. Primitive man undoubtedly avoided locations which his experience associated with sickness. In east Africa, blue gum eucalyptus trees growing beside water bodies were associated with sickness and called "fever trees" long before mosquitos were discovered to be the carriers of malaria.

> Malaria occurs throughout the world and is one of the most prevalent of all infectious diseases. In the late 1970s cases worldwide were estimated at 120 million. Hyperendemic areas are found in Central and South America, in North and Central Africa, in all countries bordering the

Mediterannean, and in the Middle East and East Asia. (*The New Encyclopaedia Britannica*, 1985)

In Pakistan and India the common delta of the Ghanges and Brahmaputra rivers has been a known focus of cholera since it was described there by a Portugese traveler in the early 16th century . . . generally confined to people of lower socioeconomic groups living in tropical and subtropical regions where there is poor sanitation. (*Encyclopedia Americana*, 1985)

Except for one space in southwest Arabia, tsetse flies and the sleeping sickness they can cause are confined to an intracontinental region in Africa extending from south of the Sahara Desert to the Republic of South Africa.

Other diseases relate "one step removed" to regions. As a nutritional disease brought about by a dietary deficiency of thiamine, beriberi is encountered most frequently in the Far East, where polished or hulled rice is a major part of the diet. Figure 38, Iodine Content of Drinking Water and Goiter Frequency, page 82, shows the regional relationships between iodine deficiency in potable water and the frequency of goiter. Occupational diseases—such as silicosis, black lung, and asbestositis—are obviously related to the areas and regions where the activities producing these environmental hazards occur.

Tropical, environmental, and space medicine illustrate academic concentrations in medical research, education, and practice that relate directly to regions. Regions are involved in the location and management of medical facilities: "burn centers" and hospitals providing other emergency or special services for a large surrounding area; or the distribution of general hospitals, convalescent homes, and public clinics with reference to the place of residence, age, and other demographic characteristics of the population within the region.

Regionalization has long been used as a means of both delivering public health services and keeping informed of health needs and potentials. Most state public health agencies are regionally organized, with the exact nature of regional responsibilities varying according to the degree

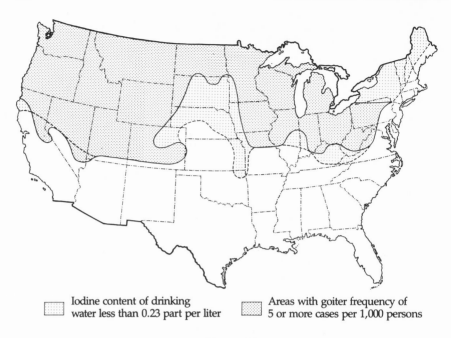

Iodine content of drinking
water less than 0.23 part per liter

Areas with goiter frequency of
5 or more cases per 1,000 persons

Figure 38
**IODINE CONTENT OF DRINKING WATER
AND GOITER FREQUENCY**
Interstate
Geology, Medicine
Research
Reference: Keller, Edward A., *Environmental Geology*, Second Edition,
Columbus, OH (Merrill), 1979, p. 336.

of public health activity of local governments. The state
health department region typically provides direct services for "unorganized" portions of its area, limited generalized service throughout the area, and serves as an
information bridge for central agency planning and operations. (Herman, 1968)

The extent to which this regionalization is realized in the organization of medical services varies widely among states,
depending on political policies and funding.

meterology   Meteorology is concerned almost exclusively with regions
since atmospheric phenomena, variations in heat and moisture, and winds occur over large areas. They do not have precise linear boundaries, they change continuously, and fluctuate

with the seasons and other environmental conditions. The weather conditions reported and the forecasts made in daily newspapers and throughout the day and night on television are expressed in regional terms (Figure 12, Weather Forecast, page 28).

> Heavy showers and thunderstorms will occur today on a 250-mile wide band from northeastern Kansas to southern Michigan. . . . Unseasonable heat will continue in the Southeast because of a high pressure area. . . . An area of showers and thunderstorms is likely in upstate New York and northern New England . . . Unsettled weather obtains in most of the Pacific Northwest and the northern Rockies. (Weather Report, 1986)

Climatology, as a subdivision of meteorology having to do with the "average course or condition of the weather at a particular place over a period of years," is concerned with large areas of the earth and its atmosphere. The earth itself is divided, of course, into tropical, temperate, and arctic zones or regions. And within these global expanses, into smaller regions according to humidity, temperature, physiography, vegetation, predominant winds, rainfall, soil types, and other characteristics. Figure 29, Avocados: Commercial Production, on page 63, is a good example of an agricultural product that can be grown commercially only within particular areas having the right microclimatic conditions, located in a few regions with the required meteorological characteristics.

The military services utilize descriptive regional information for strategic advance planning, unified regional command, and tactical operations. *military science*

> [Military] regions of the world can be identified on the basis of important similarities or differences in such broad considerations as the ease of conducting military activities, the kinds of tactics which are most feasible, or the kinds of equipment which are most appropriate. . . . From region to region there are differences in logistics requirements reflected in consumption rates, immunization requirements, protective clothing, or camouflage patterns. There are differences in the effort required in military construc-

tion, the availability of resources, the skill and number of local laborers, and the chances that useful structures exist. Other differences appear in visibility, the chances that concealed sites exist, the chances that prepared routes go in a desired direction, and the chances that routes can be organized for traffic circulation with a minimum of effort. In defining military regions such factors are very numerous. If detail is important it is useful to define military regions for special purposes such as supply allowance and distribution, military construction, tactical regions, or civil affairs regions. . . . The land of the world is roughly divisible into 40 percent cold lands, 33 percent desert and related lands, 21 percent humid tropics, and 6 percent temperate regions. These are in general the realms of arctic, desert, tropic, and normal operations. (Peltier, 1966)

The U.S. Unified Global Military Commands shown in Figure 10 on page 24 cover the entire globe except for Mexico. One of these, COMPAC, may be the largest operational region extant "responsible for maintaining security and defending US interests in an area extending from the west coast of the US to the east coast of Africa and from the Artic to the Antartic—more than half the earth's surface and home for 2 billion people living under more than a dozen flags" (*Pacific Air Forces*, 1986).

Consideration, use, and control of ground, ocean, and air space are basic in military operations and tactics. As a single example, occupation of high ground has been regarded throughout history as an advantage in military operations. To such positions on the earth's surface must now be added the much higher domain of space stations orbiting above and around the earth.

The military services make extensive use of explanatory diagrams depicting the spatial disposition and movement of armed forces on land and sea in military histories, descriptive reports, and anticipatory studies of military operations. Area, command, theater, or district are military spatial expressions equivalent to regions as discussed in this book.

The North American Air Defense Command (NORAD) is divided into seven numbered regions and the Alaskan

NORAD Region [Figure 21, page 46]. The same application
of regional concepts is demonstrated in other activities . . .
such as interceptor commands, logistics, medical, and
similar functional areas. . . . There are unified commands
. . . for large areas of the world outside the continental
United States.

To summarize, the administrative use of regional concepts to delineate areas of operational or functional
responsibility is a fundamental characteristic of Air Force
organization at all levels. (Richards, 1986)

Because most military actions do not have fixed boundaries
and are subject to rapid and repeated change, operational areas
are usually identified with a command headquarters or another
center of operations. They are nodal regions with indefinite
boundaries according to the designations adopted in this book.
In the navy, headquarters are also indefinite, moving with the
flagship of the fleet commander-in-chief operating out of the
home ports shown in Figure 39, U.S. Navy: Fleet Areas of
Responsibility, page 85.

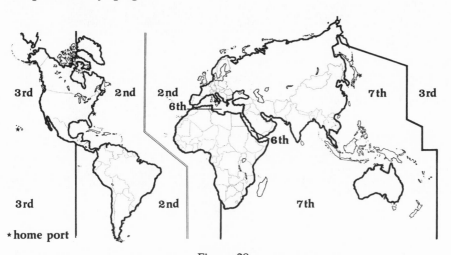

Figure 39
U.S. NAVY: FLEET AREAS OF RESPONSIBILITY
Global
Military Science
Operational
Reference: Dillon, Commander David L., USN (Director, Navy Office of
Information West, Los Angeles, CA), Personal Communication,
November 1986.

There is another set of nodal regions involved in military operations. Aircraft, naval vessels, and ground forces must function within regions determined by fuel capacity and the feasible range of logistic supply. Different types of longer range offensive and defensive weapons and equipment are effective only within their operational range or functional region. Missiles, artillery, radar, and line-of-sight communications have aerial or regional limitations (Figure 40, Radar Coverage: North American Early Warning, page 87).

Military support activities in the United States—such as recruiting, training, civil engineering, contract administration, or certain logistic supply—may be organized by region in the same way that civil government and business divide the nation into regions for decentralized administration-management purposes (Figure 16, Standard Federal Regions, page 35). For example, training and commanding the reserve forces composed of U.S. Army Reserve and National Guard units have been divided into five continental armies (CONUSAs) and a deployment force (Third Army) (Figure 41, Continental U.S. Army Commands, page 88).

oceanography   There are probably as many different kinds of regions in the vast expanse of water that covers almost three-quarters of the earth's surface as there are on dry land. Figure 13 on page 30 depicts one authority's categorization of the major Physical Regions of the Ocean. Large areas of the ocean circulate and interact with the atmosphere above, affecting the world's weather as well as marine environments.

There are dynamic regions of more localized ocean currents, such as the Gulf Stream off the eastern coast of the United States or the Peruvian current and periodic upwelling of El Niño off the western coast of South America. Tidal ranges in different regions vary from 2 to 50 feet. There are more stable regions such as the Sargasso Sea in the North Atlantic Ocean with its concentration of surface seaweeds, first reported by Christopher Columbus.

The continental shelves around the world constitute a discontinuous global region characterized by relatively shallow waters, particular vegetative and animal life, a substantial proportion of undiscovered petroleum and natural gas reserves,

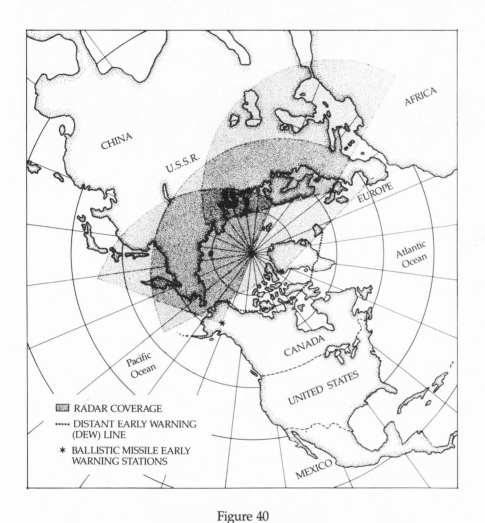

Figure 40
RADAR COVERAGE: NORTH AMERICAN EARLY WARNING
Intercontinental, International
Geography, Military Science
Planning, Operations
Reference: Weaver, Kenneth F., "Of Planes and Men, U.S. Air Force
Wages Cold War and Hot," *National Geographic*, September 1965,
pp. 314–315.

Figure 41
CONTINENTAL U.S. ARMY COMMANDS*
Intracontinental, Global
Military Science
Operational

*The Third Army (TUSA) is a regular army rapid deployment force on active duty, available for action whenever and wherever needed. Accordingly, its area of operations is a nodal region with indefinite boundaries, centered at its headquarters at Fort McPherson, Atlanta, Georgia. The indefinite outer boundaries of its nodal region are established by transport, logistics, and other operational considerations.

Reference: Los Angeles Branch, Office of the Chief of Public Affairs, Department of the Army, Personal Communication, October 1986.

extensive sand and gravel deposits, and 90 percent of the world's marine food resources. These marine food resources vary among major fishing regions: with the northeastern Atlantic, southeastern Pacific, and west central Pacific accounting for approximately 60 percent of the worldwide catch.

Certainly, the Arctic and Antarctic oceans are regions unique in their polar features affecting the climate and waters of the world as well as all human activities within arctic areas. The oceans are not only divided into regions of different average temperature horizontally between different places on the globe, but also vertically at different depths. Oceanographic exploration in recent years has revealed new regions in the ocean bottom: mid-ocean ridges resulting from the movement of tectonic plates, areas of great topographic variation, volcanic activity, and unique marine life.

Some regions of the ocean are full of background noise, underwater conditions that scatter and absorb sound, variations in temperature and density that bend and distort sound waves, and ocean rings with disruptive echoes. These acoustical differences affect the operation of exploratory and military subsurface vehicles. With nuclear powered submarines armed with nuclear missiles prowling the oceans submerged for months at a time, the reliability of acoustical detection and ranging is vital.

Pollution is a regional problem as well as a worldwide concern. Increased levels of contamination by insecticides sprayed on land have been noted in dolphins and other marine animals around the world. The Sargasso Sea is reported to accumulate plastic and other man-made material residue. Without effective regulation oil tankers dump dirty ballast before entering port. The continental shelves and coastal wetlands are regions subject to increasing land based pollution from sewage disposal, toxic runoff, industrial waste, and dumping trash, garbage, and nuclear waste in the oceans.

As the "science that deals with the life of past geological periods," paleontology is concerned with regions in at least two important ways. Fossils, the basic material of paleontological study, are found only in certain places where geological and climatological conditions or events long ago favored the   *paleontology* formation of fossils at some time in the past, and their subsequent preservation over periods ranging from thousands to several hundred million years. Two small regions where the ancestors of modern men may have originated are the west side of Lake Tarkana, formerly Lake Rudolph, in Kenya, and Olduvai Gorge in Tanzania made famous in anthropological circles by the Leaky family. Other examples of regions rich in fossil finds are the Paris and Antwerp basins, the foothills of the Alps around Belluno, Italy, and places in the Gobi Desert in Asia.

A recently discovered region, described as "one of the largest fossil finds in North America," is yielding

> thousands of fragmentary remains of primitive dinosaurs, crocodiles, sharks, and mammal-like reptiles . . . that [researchers] believe prove that a catastrophic extinction occurred 125 million years before the disappearance of dinosaurs (Sullivan, 1986). (Figure 42, Fossil Finds, page 91)

This geographical region consists of a discontinuous line of valleys which were once lakes along a rift valley extending along much of the East Coast of the United States, formed as the African lithospheric plate began to split away from the North American plate some 200 million years ago (Figure 17, Major Lithosphere Plates, page 39).

Paleontologists are also concerned with the regional environment existing at the time animate and inanimate life was fossilized. In the case of humans, what global and regional conditions existed several million years ago affecting the form, behavior, and survival of the progenitors of early men and women? In what regional environment did the dinosaurs emerge, flourish, and disappear? What regional conditions have enabled certain animal or vegetative life to survive throughout eons of time?

political
science   People's general attitudes and specific voting behavior vary on many matters according to income, age, sex, educational and marital status, employment, and religion. Areas where one or more of these characteristics predominate exhibit corresponding political predilections. For example, regions with a large proportion of their population composed of older, wealthier, married couples tend to be more conservative. Voters in

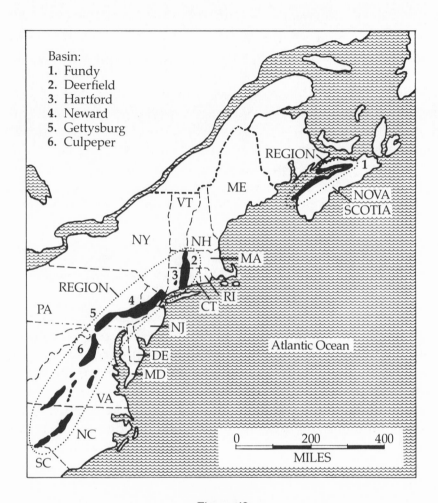

Basin:
1. Fundy
2. Deerfield
3. Hartford
4. Neward
5. Gettysburg
6. Culpeper

Figure 42
FOSSIL FINDS
Interstate
Paleontology, Geology
Discontinuous
References: Sullivan, Walter, "Before Dinosaurs, Another Catastrophe," *The New York Times*, 30 September 1986, p. 20. Olsen, Paul, E., "A 40-Million-Year Lake Record of Early Mesozoic Orbital Climatic Forcing," *Science*, 14 November 1986, 842–848.

areas of economic distress with high unemployment are not likely to favor political persons or proposals they believe will aggravate this condition.

Normally, voters who identify themselves with a particular region will resist changes that run counter to their territorial beliefs and convictions. Particular circumstances may alter this general correspondence: an exceptionally charismatic political leader, a strongly and pervasively expressed position by the state or federal government, an unexpected event of such import that it temporarily supersedes usual political reactions. However, since political considerations are part of almost all individual and collective human activity, the demographic composition of a region relates to its political attitudes. This relationship is strongest with respect to specific issues. For example, in areas where most people and the powers that be belong to one religion, political behavior is likely to reflect strong tenets of this faith. This correspondence is greatest when concurrence with higher authority is part of the faith.

In large part because of demographic characteristics, certain regions of the United States are identified as politically conservative, liberal, more or less subject to change or susceptible to inducement, opposed to or supportive of a current issue or specific proposal. Although increasingly the mass media of communication are creating and shaping more uniform attitudes and behavior, political campaigns are devised and carried out with careful attention to regional characteristics and needs.

public administration Since public administration must be concerned with politics to be effective, it relates to the regions that affect the political attitudes and behavior of the public it serves. City managers and other administrative officials are necessarily concerned with the political dynamics of the governmental jurisdiction within which they function.

Regions are employed for operational purposes. A number of the illustrations in the first chapter of this book depict areal subdivisions created for decentralized administration. This permits successful direction of an activity too complex or particular for effective management from a single headquarters. It may improve existing operations providing more efficient production and distribution of goods and services, establishing decentralized cost centers and territorial responsibilities, promoting executive development, encouraging closer grassroots contacts, or fulfilling other management purposes. (Figure 43, U.S. Internal Revenue Service, page 93)

In much the same way as other practicing professionals, public administrators make use of regional concepts to analyze and determine how best to cope with underlying situations and major problems that are not confined within municipal, county, or state boundaries and must therefore be approached regionally.

Sociology makes extensive use of the voluminous infor- *sociology* mation concerning people collected by the decennial and interim U.S. censuses. This includes data tabulated by major regional

Figure 43
U.S. INTERNAL REVENUE SERVICE
Intranational
Public Administration
Operations
Reference: *1985 Annual Report, Commissioner and Chief Counsel, Internal Revenue Service*, Washington, DC (U.S. Government Printing Office), 1985, p. 82 (updated to 1986).

subdivisions of the nation and by the many metropolitan urban
regions. Data tabulated by census tracts and states can be grouped
into regional areas best suited for special purposes.

Because of the breadth of its potential inquiry into society,
culture, social institutions, collective behavior, and social inter-
action, sociology draws on regional data formulated by various
individuals and organizations engaged in other academic fields
and operational endeavors. A number of the illustrations in
this book selected to exemplify a region associated with a field
or activity other than sociology are also relevant to human
behavior and social conditions. For example, personal ner-
vousness may relate to potential radioactive contamination or
seismic risk (Figures 11a and b, Global Contamination: Radioactive Fallout, pages 26, 27, Figure 31, Seismic Risk, page 66).
Regions of predominant religious faith influence individual
attitudes on many matters (Figure 30, Major World Religions,
page 65), and productive performance may relate to an area of
personal responsiblity (Figure 34, Automotive Manufacture:
Sales, page 71).

Sociologists have identified few regions for their own academic purposes, other than those identifying districts with particular social characteristics within metropolitan urban regions,
and studies linking certain regional characteristics with human
attitudes and behavior.

The examples of regions presented in this chapter illustrate
the wide use of the regional concept by academic fields of study
for many different purposes. Regions are interrelated in one
way or another, as is all knowledge and human endeavor. Among
the many direct and immediate interrelationships illustrated
are: seismic risk and lithosphere plates; climatic zones and deserts, rain forests, and arctic regions; regional buying power and
the marketing of products and services; airborne radioactive
fallout and weather; and operational decentralization of certain
business and military activities and physiographic regions.

One set of regions represents physical conditions or aspects
of human behavior in space. Another set depicts regions established for governmental, administration, legal, theoretical, or
other abstract purposes or parameters. Both are "real" in different ways: one with respect to the physical world of nature,
the other with respect to human institutions or mental processes.

Some of the difficulties and considerations presented for planning by the differences between these two sets of regions are examined in the next chapter.

REFERENCES

[1] Bell South, *The New York Times*, 17 February 1986, Advertisement, p. Y33. [2] Borton, Dean E., Director of Communications. Calavo Growers of California, personal communication, 3 November 1986. [3] *Encyclopedia Americana*, International Edition, Danbury CT (Grolier), 1985, Vol. 6, pp. 624–625. [4] *The Encyclopaedia Britannica*, Fourteenth Edition, Vol. 3, New York (Enclyclopaedia Britannica), 1929, p. 614. [5] Hayes, Harold T. P., "A Reporter at Large, The Last Place," *The New Yorker*, 6 December 1976, pp. 99, 55. [6] Herman, Harold (Chief of Health Planning, Office of the Surgeon General, U.S. Public Health Service), in: U.S. Department of Commerce, *Substate Districting*, Proceedings of a Technical Seminar, Annual Conference of State Planning Agencies, Washington DC (Economic Development Administration), 1968, p. 13. [7] Loomis, Robert S., "Agricultural Systems," *Scientific American*, Food and Agriculture, 1976, p. 101. [8] Museum of Natural History, Exhibit, *Late Ice-Age Art*, New York City, December 1986 (Reference: A. Leroi-Gourham, *Treasures of Prehistoric Art*, 1967). [9] *The New Encyclopaedia Brittanica*, Chicago IL (Encyclopaedia Brittanica), 1985, p. 725. [10] Pacific Air Forces, *Air Force* Magazine, May 1986, p. 96. [11] Peltier, Louis C. and G. Etzel Pearcy, *Military Geography*, Princeton NJ (Van Nostrand), 1966, p. 113. [12] Pratt, D. J., "Ecological Potential," *National Atlas of Kenya*, Nairobi, Kenya (Survey of Kenya), Third Edition, 1970, p. 28. [13] Quick, L. H., *Planning Report*, The Future World Environment, A Twenty Year Forecast, Operation Spade, Douglas Aircraft Group, Long Beach, CA, March 1966, p. 1. [14] Revelle, Roger, "The Resources Available for Agriculture," *Scientific American*, Food and Agriculture, September 1976, pp. 174, 177, 178. [15] Richards, Thomas C., Lieutenant General, USAF, Commander, Air University, U.S. Department of the Air Force, Personal Communication, 17 June 1986. [16] Rudaux, Lucien, and G. de Vaucouleurs, *Larousse Encyclopedia of Astronomy*, New York (Prometheus), 1959, pp. 377, 379. [17] Stevens, William K., "Prehistoric Society: A New Picture Emerges," *The New York Times*, 16 December 1986, p. LC1, 15. [18] Sullivan, Walter, "Before Dinosaurs, Another Catastrophe," *The New York Times*, 30 September 1986, p. Y20. [19] Vartan, Vartanig G., "Super-Regional Banks Emerge," *The New York Times*, 30 September 1985, p. Y28. [20] Weather Report, *The New York Times*, 30 September 1986, p. 16Y. [21] *Webster's New International Dictionary of the English Language*, Second Edition, Springfield, MA (Merriam), 1960, p. 115.

Concensus seems to be developing that regional (areawide) and state land use planning are both inevitable and desirable. . . . The question in not whether land use planning should transcend local government, but when and how existing statutory and institutional configurations at the state/substate, regional and local levels are to be rationized and integrated. . . . Several California statutes enable local governments to create regional and subregional planning organizations. Interestingly, however, the statutes specifically designed for the purpose have been little used. . . . the state has merely enabled local governments to act together; it has not mandated such action nor established a supervening regional authority.

Sedway/Cooke, *Land and the Environment, Planning in California Today*, 1975.

CHAPTER 3
REGIONS AND PLANNING

A S INDICATED in the last two chapters, one category of *physical regions*
regions depicts physical conditions relating to the sur-
face, subsurface, and encircling atmosphere of the earth.
They are of many types and different forms. They may portray
a situation or condition as it exists for a moment or for a near
infinity of time. They may define an area huge or small, with
boundaries that may be fixed or indefinite, zonal rather than
linear, changing irregularly, periodically within limits, or progressively. They may consist of one continuous connected
expanse or spatially separate parts. These regions may be used
for description, basic research, operational analysis, or decentralized management. In most cases they represent or reflect
realities of the physical world, with borders that may be adjusted
to coincide with jurisdictional boundaries established by man.
They may also represent spatial designations for purposes
unrelated to any physical characteristic or institutional
jurisdiction.

The second set of regions is formulated for organizational *institutional*
purposes. They are defined by humans rather than shaped by *regions*
nature. A civil government, military service, or business enterprise may designate administrative areas for its operations that
do not coincide with features on the earth but with the feasible
scope of regional management, the location of manufacturing
facilities, distribution of products, provision of services,
recruitment, or the operational range of military systems.

Institutional regions are determined by the situation and
purposes of the organization formulating them. They represent
the internal realities of the institution rather than environmental characteristics of the three-dimensional world. They may or
may not be related to spatial features. Naturally, functional

regions for flood control or water supply relate administratively to drainage basins in the first instance and sources of water in the second. The boundaries of most regions established by business to distribute a product or provide a service, or the operational range of military aircraft, do not normally coincide with geographical features.

change   Most geographic regions are slow to change, since they represent characteristics of the earth that tend to be stable. Some are subject to rapid change from natural causes: river courses under conditions favoring meander, coastlines eroded by storm waves, areas subject to seismic or volcanic forces, or deserts shifting before prevailing winds. Local weather changes rapidly, climatic regions slowly. Physical regions may be altered immediately, rapidly, or gradually by human action: topography by explosion; desertification by overgrazing or destructive agricultural practices, forests cut down for field crops, grazing, or firewood; air, water, or soil pollution; changes in the environment brought about by engineering projects of many kinds. All physical regions change continually in some way and to some extent, from natural causes or human intervention, rapidly or slowly as the case may be.

Institutional regions also vary over time. Those established by business for decentralized management may be revised for any one of many reasons: increased spatial coverage, new products or technology, competition, or changes in the number, composition, or location of the relevant population. Operational regions of the military services change with new weapons or different strategic and tactical situations. The territory covered by a civil governmental district expands or contracts as participating units are added or occasionally subtracted.

official   Unless there are active forces for change, official regions
jurisdictions tend to remain intact because their current delineation has been set by custom, prevailing practice, organized activities, and data accumulated over the years relating to their established boundaries. This is especially true for governmental jurisdictions because they are subject to several additional resistances to change. Their borders are legally constituted, rooted in history, politically or bureaucratically almost impossible to change short of war or civil turmoil. Most of the regional jurisdictions established by corporations and civil governments are bounded

by contiguous regions which are part of the same overall system of territorial subdivision. This means that several regions
are normally involved in any change in the boundaries of any
one of them. Almost always this multiple effect complicates
matters and makes change more difficult. Civil governmental
borders involve the largest number of special interests which
must be satisfied.

Institutional jurisdictions—often referred to as areas, territories, or districts—become less and less related to environmental realities as time passes. The primary problem of regional
planning is created by this discrepancy which requires cooperation among official entities for its resolution.

It is notoriously difficult to achieve intergovernmental *intergovern-*
cooperation much less close coordination. This unfortunate fact *mental*
maintains throughout the world as evidenced by history and *cooperation*
the daily news. It is one of the most serious limitations confronting the world today as primary problems become larger
in scale and more closely interrelated. The extent of the coordination needed is indicated by the regions graphically illustrated in the first chapter. Not one of them has to do with a
single governmental jurisdiction. Every one involves more than
one county, state, nation, or continent.

The problem of intergovernmental coordination is particularly difficult in the United States because of the separation
of powers between federal and state governments, and continuing disagreement or need for clarification concerning their
respective responsibilities. The Constitution reserves to the states
all powers not expressly delegated to the federal government.
Since the fifty states differ among themselves in so many ways,
national policies concerning activities that are not covered by
the Constitution develop over a period of time by a process of
public consensus and legal evolution. Direct and explicit governmental policies applying to the entire nation—relating to
land use, transportation, housing, new towns, industrialization, and other elements of regional planning—are not formulated and implemented by the federal government in the
United States as they are in many other countries.

Within the states, counties and municipalities share most
problems, public needs, and governmental activities. This is
most evident in large metropolitan urban regions where many

legally independent municipalities exist side by side, with their
jurisdictional boundaries indicated by signs identifying contiguous cities since their legal borders cannot be detected on the
ground. Often, these separate cities vary greatly in size and
character.

The average metropolitan area contains approximately
100 governments —counties, cities, towns, or townships
(in nearly half the states), school districts, and various other
special purpose districts. While approximately 100 of the
nearly 300 metropolitan areas defined by the U.S. Census
in 1980 are encompassed by only one county, the other 200
spread across two or more counties. Some of the larger
metropolitan areas have half a dozen or more counties.
Adding to the complexity of this local government fragmentation is the fact that approximately 40 metropolitan
areas cross state lines. (So, 1986)

Nowhere is the fragmentation more pronounced than
in the New York City metropolitan area, which includes
three states, hundreds of municipalities, counties, separate jurisdictions and taxing authorities. The TriState
Regional Planning Commmission, a joint agency with the
Metropolitan Regional Council, has almost 19 million people in its jurisdiction, but its limited authority is suggested
by its budget, $27,000 last year. (Herbers, John, 1978)

Integration of local governments has not been possible
because each one is reluctant to compromise "home rule" by
relinquishing any of its authority or prerogatives to an adjoining or higher public authority. There are many reasons for this.
Politicians resist giving up or sharing the powers and influence
of elective office, the appointive positions and perquisites that
normally accompany elective office, and the constituency they
have carefully nurtured. They would like to know what system
of representation is proposed for any regional integration of
existing local governments, how their political positions and
constituencies would fit into new electoral districts. Police and
fire chiefs, city attorneys, and other local government officials
and employees resist consolidation of local governments because
it would eliminate all but one of the positions they hold in

separate municipalities and counties. Certain groups fear that pensions, health plans, building and health codes, zoning, and other provisions, regulations or prerogatives that concern or interest them might be combined to their disadvantage. Under such circumstances self-interest is likely to prevail.

There are also many practical problems in consolidating police, fire, sanitation, and other local services which may have different equipment, facilities, communication systems, personnel policies, pension plans, or operating practices. It can take several years to combine some governmental services so that they function as successfully as they did before merger. On the other hand, cost savings and more efficient operations may be achieved in time by combining services. But even this worthwhile objective is frequently resisted in the real world of preference for the status quo and objection to any change that might threaten existing positions.

As shown clearly in Figure 44 on page 102, both Washington, DC and Baltimore, Maryland have spread out into the surrounding countryside during the past 30 years. So much so that they are close to forming a single physical entity, part of what some people predict will become a band of uninterrupted urban development stretching along the east coast of the United States from Boston in the north to Miami in the south. *metropolitan regional planning*

As indicated in Figure 44, the original municipal jurisdictions of Baltimore (A) and Washington (B) now comprise only a small part of the urbanized territory. The physical cities have expanded to include approximately ten times the area within the original cities, and many times their population. Two states, two capital cities, seven counties, and some forty legally independent municipalities are now part of what will soon be one continuous metropolitan region covering over 4,000 square miles.

The [Baltimore-Washington-Annapolis Area] is not a region in the sense of being a natural geographic unit, such as the Tennessee Valley. It can be viewed as a logical unit of planning only because of the dominant influence of Baltimore and Washington on physical and economic relationships with the intercity territory. The non-urban portion is frankly considered in relation to the growth of these cities. Fortunately, there are no well-established uses of

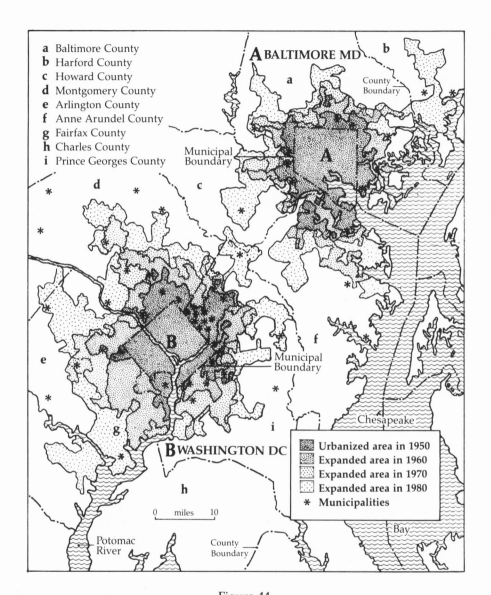

a Baltimore County
b Harford County
c Howard County
d Montgomery County
e Arlington County
f Anne Arundel County
g Fairfax County
h Charles County
i Prince Georges County

Urbanized area in 1950
Expanded area in 1960
Expanded area in 1970
Expanded area in 1980
* Municipalities

Figure 44
METROPOLITAN REGION: BALTIMORE-WASHINGTON
Interstate
Public Administration
Descriptive
Reference: *Insight*, 17 February 1986, p. 9.

land within the Area which present any conflict with this point of view. Any steps that may be taken to assure the best development of the metropolitan centers also will benefit persons living in the smaller communities and rural sections. (Maryland State Planning Commission, 1937).

Metropolitan growth has occurred around the world. Cities have grown in size and spread out spatially as people migrate to them from the countryside, and the average life expectancy of their populations increases with improved medical prevention and care. Many metropolises are much larger than the Washington-Baltimore conurbation, encompassing a proportionately larger number of governmental entities. Some spread into adjoining states or nations. Their complexity is correspondingly greater.

Our cities are becoming groups of interdependent "urban villages," which are office, industrial, retail, housing, and entertainment focal points amidst a low-density cityscape. Each urban village has its core—a kind of new downtown—where buildings are the tallest, daytime population is largest, and traffic congestion most severe. And each urban village has its outlying districts which stretch up to 10 miles from the core. (Lockwood, 1986)

Despite specific differences, the underlying situation and particular problems of metropolitan urban regions are similar. They can be generalized with the Washington-Baltimore region as an example, although it does not illustrate every situation or need of the more than 300 metropolitan areas in the United States and probably a larger number in the rest of the world.

The basic requirements of intensive human habitation are more difficult to provide in metropolitan regions composed of *basic* many separate governmental jurisdictions within one large *requirements* urbanized expanse. These requirements include a water supply for domestic, commercial, industrial, and agricultural use; a transportation system permitting the unimpeded movement of people and goods into, out of, and within the metropolitan urban area; facilities to dispose of liquid and solid wastes; storm drainage and flood control to prevent inundation; production or purchase of energy; provisions protecting the public health and maintaining environmental quality; and protection of persons and property for individual safety and social order. Economic production, financial resources, and income from various sources must make meeting these basic metropolitan requirements possible.

regional
responsibilities

Public responsibilities once identified with individual municipalities or counties separated in space become associated with the metropolitan region as these smaller governmental units coalesce into one larger urban expanse. For example, regional considerations arise when no-growth legislation is enacted unilaterally by a city or county within a metropolitan urban area.

> In regions with expanding populations, a city's or county's decision to limit growth usually forces another part of the region to pay the price—in greater densities, higher prices, more pollution, more sprawl. By forcing cities and counties to offer concrete reasons to justify policies which, on their surface, may seem inimical to the greater regional welfare, state law seeks to thwart jurisdictions' selfish attempts to enrich or protect themselves at their neighbor's expense. (Abbott, 1986)

Laws which require cities and counties to assume their "fair share" of metropolitan needs can apply to new housing construction, air pollution regulation, water quality control, waste disposal, and other actions that may impose an undue obligation or pressure on neighboring local governments.

Since some effects of every action extend far and wide in today's world of myriad interrelationships, some spatial limitation on the external impact of local ordinances must be established. For example, it would be analytically impossible and operationally impractical to relate self-imposed housing limitations in one municipality to the availability of housing in another town several hundred miles away.

The areal considerations mandated in state legislation are not defined specifically because they are different depending on the subject and situation. Fair-share housing—which divides the responsibility of providing low cost housing proportionately among the municipalities within the metropolitan urban area—involves regions of various sizes depending on the characteristics, growth rate, and disposition in space of the population. Air pollution usually relates to large airshed expanses. Water contamination may cover large or small areas, depending on the geographical and geological situation, and the location and characteristics of the sources of water pollution. The environmental economic impacts on regional planning of unilateral actions by individual governments within the urbanized area change as conditions change.

The validity and usefulness of regions as a basis for distributing responsibility among the governments affected depends on the extent to which these governments follow the spirit rather than the letter of the law requiring apportionment. This is because such a law cannot assign specific quotas or prescribe a precise method of calculating proportional responsibility without imposing what would be regarded today as a politically unacceptable restriction of local rights or "home rule." And no local government wants to take the initiative in limiting its own actions for regional reasons without comparable commitments from other governments within the area.

Only upon appeal to the courts will failure by local governments to consider repercussive regional effects be corrected as case law develops gradually defining more precisely their respective responsibilities. This is likely to take some time because only a small percentage of those adversely affected by irresponsibly self-centered city planning laws can afford to appeal injurious consequences to the courts.

> Policy in the United States is directed toward the solution of specific problems, wherever they arise, rather than toward securing some kind of theoretically desirable 'balance' between or within whole 'regions' (Organization for Economic Co-operation and Development, 1980).

At present, to the extent possible, fundamental metropolitan needs are met by the regular operating units of the municipalities and counties within the urbanized area: police, fire, sanitation, traffic and transportation, public works, health services and other units of local government. There is professional and technical cooperation between different jurisdictions when this benefits each participant. Larger local governmental units may contract to provide essential services for nearby jurisdictions which cannot supply them efficiently for themselves because of their small size, without raising taxes substantially.

Many public officials say there is no better example of what local government may be like in the future than in Palm Beach County, where much of the growth in southeast Florida has occurred in recent years. . . .

County government, in effect, has been superimposed over a complex matrix of jurisdictions. These include 37 municipalities ranging from tiny villages to coastal cities . . . 20 or 50 separate special districts that provide such services as land drainage and soil conservation, and scores of private residential developments that have never been incorporated but provide such basic services as fire and police protection. . . .

*special
districts*

County governments—not cities, towns, the states, or the federal Government—frequently have the chief responsibility for providing the streets, bridges, engineering and other resources needed to end the [traffic] chaos. . . . In New York [state] . . . counties have become the delivery system for almost every human service program. . . .

The rising level of authority held by county government . . . was not the result of any formal transfer of powers. Rather, it came as new population growth forced the unincorporated areas and smaller governments, including the cities, to turn to the counties for assistance. (Herbers, 1987)

The special district is widely employed as a means of providing a single public service for local governments which cannot supply the service themselves or could do so only at great cost. Water supply is a notable example. Few large cities can meet their water needs from sources within their respective jurisdictions. Water must be imported to most metropolitan urban regions, often from considerable distances requiring large capital expenditures. This is performed most successfully by a water district formed by a number of local governments combining their financial resources, each obtaining an agreed-upon share of the water imported. The Metropolitan Water District of Southern California described in the next chapter is a specific example.

There are more than 25,000 special districts in the United States providing a wide range of services, each with its board of directors, governors, or commissioners. They have the power to tax, issue revenue bonds, or impose special fees collected for them by local governments; this avoids the increase in the general tax rate which usually means defeat at the next election for legislators identified with the tax increase. As many as 1,000 of these districts supply entire metropolitan urban regions with water, energy, storm drainage, sewerage, public transportation, or some other essential service. Most cover smaller areas providing a variety of services such as additional fire protection or street lighting. Special districts are also found in the countryside for flood control, soil conservation, irrigation, health services, grazing, agricultural adjustment, and other rural needs.

Another means of metropolitan coordination and planning are councils of government (COGs). *councils of government*

> [They] are permanent organizations with a voluntary membership composed of local governments interested in achieving a degree of metropolitan planning and coordinated operations. They are supported by grants from various federal departments and agencies in connection with programs they are sponsoring at the local level, and by dues collected from participating local governments. . . . They correlate local requests for federal funding with existing commitments within the metropolitan area, the plans of constituent governments, and the COGs' own formulation of desirable area wide development. . . . They cannot collect taxes, enact ordinances, or require implementing legislation or other actions by local government within the metropolitan region. Besides their function of generating voluntary coordinated planning and reviewing requests for federal aid, [the most successful COGs] serve as centers of regional information and analysis, provide a means of pooling resources, and act as a focus for the discussion and resolution of metropolitan issues and projects. (Branch, 1985)

special   In the United States special arrangements provide varying
arrangements degrees of metropolitan urban planning in a few places. Some
municipalities and surrounding counties have merged to enlarge
the area subject to operational coordination and planning. A
few cities annexed enough surrounding territory to comprise
a small metropolitan region. One medium size city has formed
a metropolitan council, another a special metropolitan service
district; both are advisory in nature, with limited responsibilities for planning and providing public services.

     The scope of activities of regional agencies has broad-
ened. Over the past decade, many of them have added
economic development, transportation, housing, human
services, management assistance, and computer services
to their basic roster of land-use planning and environmental protection concerns. (McDowell, 1984)

planning   Neither separately nor collectively do the operations of civil
comprehensive governments, special districts, or regional agencies constitute
comprehensive planning for metropolitan urban areas. Inte-
grated planning of all governmental activities for an entire urban
area and sufficient surrounding territory to accommodate population growth and spatial expansion has not been achieved in
the United States. Nor has comprehensive planning been
attained at higher levels of civil government for their territorial
jurisdictions, for the same reasons that have made it impossible
in metropolitan regions. County, state, and federal legislative
bodies and chief executive officials are unable or unwilling to
integrate the operations of the different departments and agencies that constitute each of these levels of government.

     Business and the military services can plan comprehen-
sively on a regional basis as they see fit because their activities
are narrower in scope and subject to greater executive authority
than civil government. At best, they are concerned only indirectly with the range of societal considerations and public
responsibilities for which civil government is directly account-
able to the electorate.

     Since the simplest activities consist of multiple parts, they
can be planned comprehensively if all their primary parts are
taken into account; no crucial component is unrecognized or
ignored. Without this inclusive view, planning is partial and

less likely to be successful. Comprehensive planning can be applied to the entire organization, at every level of management, and to each of its separate parts. But in this book, the term refers to planning at the highest directorial level of the organization, top management, rather than to one of its subordinate subsystems or component functions.

Global air transportation is an impressive example of comprehensive planning of a complex activity by business and government which includes aircraft design, manufacture, operation, maintenance, and replacement; airport design, construction, and management; worldwide communications; flight operations and control conducted in a common language; reservations and ticketing; safety regulations and accident investigation.

The intercontinental ballistic missile and nuclear submarine forces could not function without skillful comprehensive planning of the people, weapons, communication and command, maintenance, training, supply, and support which together comprise these global military systems. Command of an aircraft carrier requires comprehensive planning of its primary force of as many as 85 aircraft, other weapons systems, a crew of some 5,000 men and women, and the operation of the ship itself—not to mention taking into account weather conditions, friendly forces, and hostile actions or intentions.

The next step in the sequence of effective planning involves *subsystems* a group of elements that are sufficiently interrelated to form a subsystem within the total organization, managed or commanded by one person.

The components of the missile and submarine forces noted above are subsystems within a large region of the world under a "unified global military commander" (Figure 10, page 24). In turn, this area of command is a subsystem from the viewpoint of a commander-in-chief and combined general staff responsible for planning and operations around the globe.

Well managed local governments regard energy supply as a subsystem: adjusting their generation or purchase of energy among available sources according to the comparative cost of coal, oil, natural gas, nuclear fuel, wind and water power, firewood in parts of the world, existing production and distribution systems, and present and projected demand for energy.

Large corporations often group related operations in one organizational unit composed of several smaller components, under one executive. For example, if the company manufactures several makes of automobiles or other products similar in nature, the separate units may be associated in one manufacturing subsystem. Or sales, marketing, and advertising departments might be grouped as a division because of their close interrelationships. Such subsystems are shown clearly in corporate organization charts. They may improve efficiency in several ways. Certain production processes are shared by the different units of the subsystem, avoiding duplication. The price of parts, materials, and supplies is reduced when they are purchased in larger quantities. Distributors or service outlets may be able to handle several related products or services. The managerial span of control is reduced and the chain of reporting and command simplified.

functional   Functional planning relates to a particular element or activity, one of the multiple activities involved in all human endeavors. Different units of local government plan their respective operations: supplying water, police and fire protection, constructing public works, providing health services, controlling traffic, or some other public service. In business, functional planning is performed by different components of the organization for their particular area of expertise and responsibility: product design, operations, sales, storage, distribution, or advertising.

> Scanners, those computerized devices that record product details in supermarkets and retail stores, are causing an upheaval in merchandising. . . . The use of scanning data now provides a direct measurement of sales effort . . . analyzing segments of the regional market, such as how many people in Detroit prefer tuna canned in water to tuna canned in oil. . . . "The big shift is to regional marketing because now the data are available to do it." (Fowler, 1986)

> At American Telephone & Telegraph Co's Bedminster, N.J. Network Operations Center, the heart of the long-

distance network . . . console managers sitting at computer terminals are monitoring phone traffic by watching
a 14-by-10 foot surveillance board listing AT&T's switching
centers.

Suddenly . . . the console manager watching for facility
outages, gets a call from the Chicago regional center. A
coaxial cable in Cincinnati is down and phone service on
as many as 10,000 lines could be affected.

The seven regional centers reporting to the operations
center . . . begin rerouting traffic around Cincinnati.
(Guyon, 1986)

Functional planning is conducted within each military service by its recruitment, training, supply, maintenance, medical,
and other support units, and by each unit in a combat command for its designated operations.

The administrative situation that arises when there are
numerous regions performing different functions, many with
different boundaries and office locations, is illustrated in Figure
45 on page 112. The pattern is somewhat simplified because
the borders of a number of the administrative regions of these
six California state agencies coincide along the major mountain
ranges on two sides of the Central Valley. Nonetheless, this
sample of six demonstrates that the boundaries of the 50 or
more functional regions in California comprise a complex pattern of managerial responsibilities and operational activities.
In a smaller state without the predominant geographical feature in central California shown clearly in Figure 27 on page
55, the network of territorial boundaries would be even more
spatially diverse and complicated. Correlation of the data accumulated over the years referring to these various regions requires
statistical adjustment between the different areas they cover.
And where regional offices are located in different places, communication between them in person is made more difficult.

Growth in the number of planning districts with different geographical boundaries has created a barrier to
coordinated and integrated planning, particularly in gathering and sharing data, assessment of citizen needs, and
availability of resources outside the boundaries of individ-

ual programs. Such barriers have been created among agencies planning in different but related functional areas, as well as among agencies planning the same functional areas. (Controller of the United States, 1977)

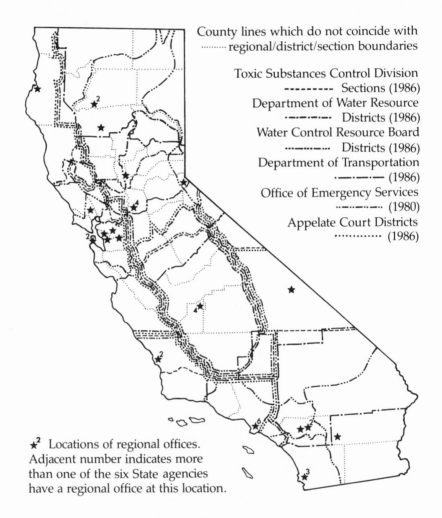

County lines which do not coincide with
········· regional/district/section boundaries

Toxic Substances Control Division
--------- Sections (1986)
Department of Water Resource
·—·—·—· Districts (1986)
Water Control Resource Board
··—··—··— Districts (1986)
Department of Transportation
·—·—·— (1986)
Office of Emergency Services
··—··—··· (1980)
Appelate Court Districts
············ (1986)

★² Locations of regional offices.
Adjacent number indicates more
than one of the six State agencies
have a regional office at this location.

Figure 45
REGIONAL BOUNDARIES AND OFFICES:
SIX CALIFORNIA STATE AGENCIES
Intrastate
Public Administration
Descriptive
References: Descriptive publications of the agencies listed above.

Planning is applied to intangible processes as well as tangible products: personnel policies and practices, recruitment and training, organizational advancement, working conditions, prerequisites, or cash flow. The arrangement of administrative units within organizations is planned: their respective responsibilities, interrelationships, and the chain of decision making or military command. Legislation, regulatory requirements, executive directives, and administrative instructions incorporate planning in their conceptualization and precise formulation, as well as in the initial determination of the results they are intended to produce.

Regional concepts and the specific designation of regions for various purposes are employed in comprehensive, subsystem, and functional planning in many ways illustrated in the previous and following chapters.

By no means is all planning desirable as drawn, or successful when completed. It is subject to the same inadequacies and the same disruptive events as any other human activity. Many plans are ill-conceived, misguided, or poorly programmed in the first place. Some do not work out because certain conditions incorporated in the plan that are prerequisite to its success may change unexpectedly before implementation of the plan is undertaken. Since most plans require at least several years to complete, unexpected developments can occur during their effectuation which necessitate immediate revision.

Probably the largest number of unsuccessful plans are those that profess or imply that they will resolve the problem or complete the project proposed, but in fact the formulators of these plans know that they can achieve the proposed purpose only in part. Usually this is because elected officials and chief executives are unwilling to "bite the bullet" with plans that are drawn to meet the need completely; they fear that the policy commitment or allocation of funds required could jeopardize re-election or bring formal disapproval or dismissal. Most civil governmental plans are of this type. They are not successful to the extent that they do not attain the stated or presumed objective nor meet the real need because they were not intended to do so in the first place.

Like most human misadventures planning failures are rarely acknowledged and are usually forgotten as soon as possible.

unsuccessful

No one likes to admit error, to oneself much less to others. Accordingly, there are few analytical studies of planning mistakes intended to forestall similar blunders in the future.*

In civil government in the first half of this century numerous city plans for land use were produced in a year or two by outside consultants and delivered to municipal bureaucracies which did not participate in their formulation and considered them inadequate or unrealistic. As a consequence, most of them were ignored, soon outdated, and never realized.

Fifteen years ago, the U.S. Department of Housing and Urban Development guaranteed mortgages for the purchase of large tracts of land by private enterprise to construct thirteen new towns. Grants were made for the preparation of master plans for these new communities, which were to contain business, industry, and an economically and socially balanced resident population. Most of these new towns were never built; not one was completed as planned. The federal government acknowledged its failure of planning policy and procedure by withdrawing completely from the endeavor.

> In 1970, the Brazilian government announced plans to integrate the Amazon region with the rest of the country. The forest-clad region was to be crisscrossed by a web of pioneer roads with the east-west Transamazon Highway serving as the backbone for the system . . . designed to accomplish three main goals . . . a safety valve for the poverty-stricken Northeast . . . fill a demographic void in a region occupying half of Brazil's territory but containing only 4 percent of the nation's population . . . create access to mineral and timber reserves. . . .
>
> The Transamazon scheme has largely failed on all three counts . . . [after spending] close to $500 million . . . with little or no understanding of the ecological and cultural conditions of settlements. (Smith, 1981)

> The seeds of [another] mistake—which the planners themselves admit was a classic of its kind—were sown during the Arab oil embargo. The Saudi government, fear-

---

*One exception is a book discussing six examples of what the author considers badly misguided planning (Hall, 1980).

ing that wheat-producing countries might retaliate for the oil shortages, decided to forestall wheat shortages at home by encouraging domestic production. . . . [Farmers] produced so much of the world's most expensive wheat last year that Saudi Arabia couldn't eat it all. . . . In fact, the Saudis couldn't even store all the wheat. . . . Planners are wondering how long the government can keep supporting the farmers so generously. In addition, planners are increasingly worried about draining the underground aquifers. In this desert country without any rivers, Saudi Arabia's new five-year development plan portrays a parched future. It estimates that agriculture now consumes 84% of the water used and that 70% of that comes from aquifers that aren't naturally replenished. (Rosewicz, 1986)

Business also has its failures. Bankruptcies bear witness to poor planning in many instances, as well as to damaging developments, extraordinary conditions, or disastrous events no one could anticipate. Since by its nature business involves more opportunism and risk taking than civil government and the military services in peacetime, a higher percentage of plans that do not succeed can be expected—although characteristic optimism may make this difficult for business men and women to acknowledge. New products are conceived, carefully planned, and test marketed, but fail. Companies are merged or acquired with the best intentions for desirable diversification or vertical integration of production, to be separated several years later because the plan did not work out. Large successful companies are not immune.

I.B.M. and Merrill Lynch announced the end of the project in a four sentence release. . . . With yesterday's announcement Immet joins a long list of home and office information services that have failed in recent years. Last month CBS, Inc. pulled out of Trintex. . . . Knight-Ridder, Inc., the newspaper publisher, abandoned its $50 million videotex effort. . . . The Times Mirror Company and the Centel Corporation also abandoned their offerings in southern California and Chicago. . . . A recent review of a study, started at I.B.M.'s instigation, had concluded that "the project would not be profitable for a long, long time, and might never be profitable at all." (Sanger, 1987)

In 1952, United States Steel, now U.S.X., wasted $500 million on an open-hearth plant just as Japanese and European rivals were shifting to far more efficient oxygen furnaces. . . .

General Motors, which acquired H. Ross Perot's Electronic Data Systems and Mr. Perot with it, paid him $743 million to go away and stop criticizing G.M. management. (Lekachman, 1987)

Whether a military plan is sound or faulty cannot be judged by its success if the enemy has superior military resources or an act of God intervenes. When withdrawal or stalemate is out of the question, plans must still be drawn by the weaker antagonist for a successful defense or even victory, although there is little chance that either outcome can be achieved. Certainly, as an example of great magnitude and far-reaching consequences, French military plans before World War II which relied on the Maginot Line and static defense proved disastrous when confronted with the fluid strategy and blitzkrieg tactics of the German forces. Iraq's attack on Iran when it was disrupted after the fall of the Shah in 1980 did not lead to sudden victory as planned but to a long regional war which has lasted many years with heavy casualties. Cancellations of weapons systems by the military establishment in the United States —after years of research, development, prototype testing, and the expenditure of hundreds of millions of dollars—represent failures of planning.

DIVAD cost the taxpayers 1.8 billion dollars, yet it was destined to be the antiaircraft gun that couldn't.

It couldn't shoot far enough to hit tank-killing helicopters; couldn't keep up with the tanks it was supposed to protect; couldn't track low-flying targets, climb hills or cross ditches—and wouldn't start on cold mornings.

On August 27 [1985] the supersophisticated air-defense gun became the first major weapons system scrubbed by the Reagan administration. (*U.S. News*, 1985)

[The Pentagon's own Inspector General] and his staff have conducted audits of the [Defense Systems Acquisition Review Council's] decisions on 16 different weapons programs. He found that its members routinely ignore Defense Department regulations, rarely scrutinize a weapon during the early stages of its development, frequently fail to demand detailed information about a weapon's defects, and rarely demand an explanation for delays. . . . (Smith, 1985)

A proportion of all plans drawn by any organization will   *prospects* not be carried out in whole or in part. If successful realization of plans as drawn must be almost guaranteed, only plans with very limited objectives would be proposed and their implementation undertaken. The fact that planning has been successful more often than unsuccessful is evidenced by the historical development of civilization in both its constructive and destructive aspects. Examples of effective regional planning of different kinds and spatial scope constitute the next chapter.

The quality and reliability of functional and subsystem planning have advanced in recent years because of the general acceleration of knowledge. More and more is being revealed concerning the interrelationships among natural phenomena and among human activities, and between these two sets of interactions. Increasingly, the separate functional activities that comprise subsystems can be correlated for maximum collective output.

At the same time, instant communications and ever closer economic, political, and social ties between people and places near and far are complicating matters by multiplying the number of factors that must be taken into account in planning. Nowadays legislative bodies, business executives, and military commanders are confronted with organizations and activities that are becoming increasingly complex and sensitive to internal and external events.

It is at the highest level of responsibility and decision mak-   *difficulties* ing that effective planning and operational integration are most difficult to achieve. Not many years ago most chief executives believed they could evaluate and act constructively without the analytical support of a comprehensive planning staff. Because the activities of civil governments, businesses, and the military services were simpler years ago, decision makers could rely on their own capabilities without assistance to a much greater extent than is possible today when human affairs are not only more complicated but more specialized.

Some chief executives still find it difficult to acknowledge the usefulness of a staff to provide the information and analysis for planning purposes they do not have the time to develop for themselves. The exceptional self-confidence or aggressiveness normally required to attain high office may increase the reluctance of top managers to accept staff assistance. Also, direct and active engagement in comprehensive planning adds to the burden of responsibilities and demands on their time imposed on most chief executives. Elected officials would like to avoid the commitments required in comprehensive planning that may be uncontroversial at the time they are made, but become a liability at re-election time if voter attitudes have changed. Although corporate executives do not face the public electorate, they must satisfy their board of directors, their customers, and stockholders. Military commanders must have the confidence of their superiors whose periodical evaluation of their performance will in large part determine promotion to higher rank.

Comprehensive planning is by its nature difficult to conduct and to apply. It requires time, much thought, and extra effort, which most people willingly undertake only if they believe it necessary, compellingly desirable, or in their own self-interest. Organizational units subordinate to higher authority resist comprehensive planning at a higher level of management or command if they believe it will impose restraints on their freedom of choice and action. Most individuals and organizations would like greater independence than conditions and requirements in the real world normally permit.

These are some of the reasons that comprehensive planning has not yet been introduced at the highest directive levels of civil government in the United States, where the range of required consideration and decision is most crucial and the implications for society greatest. It is only in the past 25 years that comprehensive corporate planning has been formalized as part of top management in many business enterprises. And it is only recently that unified global military commands have been established and the Joint Chiefs of Staff reorganized so that the chairman is responsible for integrating the inputs of each military service into a unified report and comprehensive recommendations for the commander-in-chief. Legislation proposed by the House Armed Services Committee would

> "focus the peacetime military on its wartime missions and responsibilities". . . . by giving regional commanders . . . total authority over forces assigned to them, regardless of whether the units are part of the Army, Navy, or Air Force. . . .
>
> This authority would extend to such matters as discipline and training . . . to assign and dismiss commanders of the principal units under his command and to prescribe the chain of command within his region.
>
> The House panel's proposal would even give the combat commanders a budgetary account of their own, outside of the budgets for each individual military service. . . .
>
> The commanders would also play a more significant role in advising the civilian leaders of the Pentagon about how to allocate funds for particular weapons within the over-all military budget. (Cushman, 1986)

To the difficulties inherent in the comprehensive planning process discussed above must be added the need to relate many plans to natural regions on the ground and in the atmosphere. Early humans, like their animal predecessors and contemporaries, knew no jurisdictional boundaries other than those they may have marked to designate the territory they required for hunting, food gathering, and other activities essential to their survival. As civilization advances and human activities expand in number and complexity, societal organizations multiply and the number of governmental units and jurisdictional boundaries of many kinds increases. There are now several hundred thousand civil governmental units in the United States: municipalities, school districts, special districts, service areas, counties, and states. Underneath this maze of boundary lines is another maze designating property ownerships. Very few of the myriad boundaries of these jurisdictions coincide by chance or by intent with natural regions or with those established for management purposes.

The anachronism of geographical subdivisions in this
country must be changed. . . . Does it make sense for air
pollution control policy to stop at either side of the Hudson
River? Does it make sense for mass transit policy to be
intercepted by the arbitrary boundaries of New York City
and Westchester County? Does it make sense for the economic viability of the region to have to involve the coming
together of sovereign jurisdictions, often unable to agree
on rational policy that would benefit them all. . .? (Golden,
1975)

Resources are being wasted by boundary, jurisdictional
and program frictions which need not exist, and areawide
needs simply are going unmet for the lack of effective
regional units authorized to meet them. (Merriam, 1978)

need   Regions are becoming more significant for various reasons.
Much has been learned in the past several decades concerning
the regional character of the earth and its environment. Remote
sensing from orbiting satellites and high flying aircraft has
revealed new geographical and geological regions, and added
more detailed or exact information about known regions. People are more aware of environmental conditions as they affect
the habitat of humans and other animate life. In general, expansion of fact gathering, statistical reporting, and electronic computer analysis has refined the identification of regions relating
to human behavior and attitudes. Environmental contamination, severe droughts, and civil disorder are among the more
dramatic of the geographical, economic, social, and cultural
differences that exist among regions, affecting their current
condition and future prospects.
     Significant events are announced to the world at large in a
matter of days if not minutes. Highly developed communication systems have permitted great expansion of the organizational size and geographical scope of private enterprise and
military activities. The number of businesses operating at a
global, intercontinental, and international level has risen dra-
matically in recent years. More and more products large and
small are produced and marketed in different parts of the world.
Advances in long range aircraft, intercontinental ballistic missiles, orbiting space satellites, and troop and cargo airlift have

expanded the range of military strategy and operations. New regions have been created and existing regions have been accentuated by new knowledge and exceptional events. The growth of metropolitan urban agglomerations around the world has certainly focused attention and concern on these places, particularly in industrially developing nations where metropolitan concentrations have been most pronounced.

The relevance and benefits of comprehensive planning are increased when the regional concept is successfully incorporated in the process. At the same time it makes planning more difficult by adding another element of consideration, analysis, and implementation. The difficulties of relating regions to jurisdictional boundaries must be overcome. This will be hardest for civil government because of the deeply rooted association of state, county, and municipal borders with political independence. Regions have always been part of business analysis, production, and distribution. The military services consider regions in their peacetime operations and plans directed at a potential adversary; at the same time they must carefully honor national borders dividing friend and foe.

The best planning incorporates regional factors in the analytical process when they are part of the planning problem and its resolution. First considered are those representing the realities of the physical world: the location of natural and man-made features, the disposition of flora and fauna, and animate and inanimate forces. On this background descriptive of the underlying physical world is superimposed the second set of spatial delineation depicting political jurisdictions, demographic facts, real property ownerships, and the operating boundaries of any organizations and institutions to be taken into account.

Planning analysis seeks a solution to the problem at hand which coincides rather than conflicts with these sets of areas and regions. Planning is most effective over time when it supports rather than contradicts regional realities.

At present, comprehensive consideration of regions in planning in the United States is possible in business and most recently by the combined military services. It is not now applied by civil governments since they do not yet conduct comprehensive planning at the highest level of decision making. When this most important form of planning is attained at each of the three levels of government, their plans will be formulated and applied in closer coincidence with regions than is now possible. And comprehensive planning by the military services will be fully realized when each service defers its separate best interest in favor of better performance in combined operations; implicit in this process is thorough consideration of regions in contingency plans and operations orders.

The clear and present need for effective comprehensive planning formulated and applied with reference to regions is becoming a pressing necessity as technological and economic developments accentuate the regional nature of the real world.

REFERENCES

[1] Abbott, William, esq., "Land Use Litigation News," *California Planner*, April/May 1986, p. 3. [2] Branch, Melville C., *Comprehensive City Planning, Introduction and Explanation*, Chicago, IL (American Planning Association), 1985, pp. 194, 195. [3] Controller of the United States, *Federally Assisted Areawide Planning: Need to Simplify Policies and Practices*, Washington DC (General Accounting Office), 1977, p. 41. [4] Cushman, John H., Jr., "House Bill Seeks Military Changes," *The New York Times*, 16 June 1986, p. Y11. [5] Fowler, Elizabeth M., "Scanners Changing Marketing," *The New York Times*, 28 October 1986, p. Y29. [6] Golden, Harrison J. (former Controller of New York City), *Princeton Alumni Weekly*, 1 December 1975, p. 9. [7] Guyon, Janet, "A Switch in Time, Keeping the calls flowing at AT&T's long-distance network headquarters," *The Wall Street Journal*, 24 February 1986, Section 4, p. 80. [8] Hall, Peter, *Great Planning Disasters*, Berkeley, CA (University of California Press), 1982, 308 pp. [9] Herbers, John, "Deep Government Disunity Alarms Many U.S. Leaders," *The New York Times*, 11 December 1978, p. 74. [10] _____, "Counties Acquire New Burdens and Powers," *The New York Times*, 10 June 1987, p. Y1. [11] Lekachman, Robert, "Competition Is Dead, Long Live Competition," *The New York Times*: Book Review, New York (The New York Times), 11 January 1987, p. 10. [12] Lockwood, Charles, "The Arrival of the Urban Village," *Princeton Alumni Weekly*, 26 November 1986, p. 11. [13] McDowell, Bruce D., "Regions Under Reagan," *Planning*, August 1984, p. 25. [14] Maryland State Planning Commission, *Regional Planning*, Part IV, Baltimore-Washington-Annapolis Area, Baltimore MD, November 1937, p. 1. [15] Merriam, Robert E. (Chairman, Advisory Commission on Intergovernmental Relations) in: Herbers, John, "Deep Government Disunity Alarms Many U.S. Leaders," *The New York Times*, 11 December 1978, p. 74. [16] Organization for Economic Co-operation and Development, *Regional Policies in the United States*, Paris, France, 1980, p. 12. [17] Rosewicz, Barbara, "Saudi Arabia Battles a Glut, but It Isn't the One You

Think," *The New York Times*, 2 April 1986, p. 1. [18] Sanger, David E., "Merrill, I.B.M. End Venture," *The New York Times*, 1 January 1987, pp. Y21, 34. [19] Smith, Nigel J. H., "Colonization Lessons from a Tropical Forest," *Science*, 13 November 1981, pp. 755, 760. [20] Smith, R. Jeffrey, "Pentagon Decision-Making Comes Under Fire," *Science*, 4 January 1985, p. 32. [21] So, Frank, Irving Hand, and Bruce D. McDowell (Editors), *The Practice of State and Regional Planning*, Chicago, IL (American Planning Association), 1986, p. 133. [22] Unwin, Sir Raymond, *Housing & Town Planning, 1936—Lectures—1937*, New York (Columbia University), undated, p. 85. [23] *U.S. News*, "After a Big Gun Comes Up a Dud," 9 September 1985, p. 11.

There is a growing awareness of the need for regional planning in many countries. . . . However skillful the approach of the regional planner and however efficient the regional machinery, regional problems will persist for many years to come. But the failure to tackle them now, and with vigor, will result in even greater social, economic, and political problems in the future.

John Glasson, *An Introduction to Regional Planning, Concepts, Theory and Practice*, 1978.

PART 2
PRACTICE

Almost all [civil governmental] regional organizations face major difficulties in implementing their plans. They could use greater authority, more stable organizational structures and financial resources, stronger linkags with other regional organizations, more consistent support from a wide variety of federal aid programs, and stronger support from and linkages to state governments. But all of these are hard to come by. Still, great progress was made between 1965 and 1980. Regional problems and regional organizations are likely to become even more important and more effective in the decades ahead, despite the federal withdrawal from regional activities.

Bruce D. McDowell, *The Practice of State and Regional Planning*, 1986.

CHAPTER 4

REGIONAL PLANNING IN PRACTICE

THE EXAMPLES of regions presented in this book confirm the great diversity in their use. Basically, however, they are employed in one of several ways. They may delineate physical conditions or socioeconomic situations on earth. They may indicate areas of administrative supervision or other managerial direction. Or, they may be designated as territories to be developed socioeconomically, physically, or in some particular way by the adoption of policies and the instigation of actions to a desired end. Regions are a means of analytical description, administrative organization, or management direction. They are also an object of deliberate change.

This chapter illustrates various ways regions are used in planning and operations in practice. Specific examples are presented beginning with the military services, followed by business, and ending with civil government as the institutional activity most crucial for society and civilization. These examples include single-purpose, multi-purpose, and comprehensive planning at different levels of application: global, international, national, and intranational. Some illustrations are selected from countries outside the United States in order to emphasize the worldwide applicability and use of the regional concept.

In the civil government category the example of comprehensive planning in the United States is a best effort in "urban and regional planning," rather than truly comprehensive planning which as noted in the previous chapter has not yet been achieved in this country. No example of global civil governmental planning is given since none can exist in the world as it is now politically constituted.

127

Military Services

Five different regions employed by the U.S. armed forces were used in previous chapters to illustrate different types of areal coverages; they also exemplify the use of military regions in practice.

command Unified global military commands are regions within which army, navy, air force, or marine flag officers command all military personnel in all military services in their theater of operations (Figure 10, page 24). They are responsible for comprehensive planning and unified military operations throughout a geographically extensive jurisdiction, subject only to directives from higher authority.

The North Atlantic Treaty Organization (NATO) is an international cooperative regionalization of western European military forces.

The U.S. Navy's fleet areas of responsiblility (Figure 39, page 85) define the geographical jurisdiction of fleet commanders for their operational subsystem within the larger global system directed by the Chief of Naval Operations in Washington. Their military domain includes a fleet headquarters, combat vessels of various types, several kinds of aircraft, support vessels, materiel, communications, military and civilian personnel, and shore installations.

air defense As a subsystem of air force operations as a whole, the North American Air Defense (NORAD) is organized into regions fitting its tactical purposes, which require planning and operational coordination of such components as early warning, search and intercept, combat tactics, aircraft maintenance and readiness, materiel, communications, and personnel (Figure 21, page 46).

training Training and related operations of the military reserve forces
reserve of the U.S. army reserve and national guard units have been divided into five armies within the continental United States, each operating within a regional area from a regional headquarters (Figure 41, page 88). The nodal region of the rapid deployment force based in Atlanta, Georgia, has a temporary headquarters and indefinite boundaries until it is deployed in the field somewhere in the world.

early The regional coverage and single-purpose performance of
warning early warning military radar systems depends on the location

of the radar equipment, its transmissive power, and topo-graphical conditions creating blind spots, echoes, or other "noise" (Figure 40, page 87).

Regional decentralization to optimize attainment of a spe-cific objective is illustrated by military recruitment. All four of the military services recruit at the local level. They have con-cluded that organizational decentralization is desirable for their particular function within the total military system. *recruitment*

Decentralization permits the personal contact between recruiters and applicants or potential candidates that is required for success. Operations can be tailored to fit the demography of the population within feasible travel range of each recruiting center, not only as the population pool exists today but accord-ing to reliable projections of the changes among different age groups that will occur in the future. Rewarding relationships can be established at the local level with the educational and other institutions within the recruiting area which provide many of the recruits.

Intimate knowledge of the recruitment market developed in these ways permits fitting public relations activities, announcements, and advertising to the population groups, organizations, attitudes, and aspirations that experience shows produce the best results. Accumulating and maintaining this experience in the form of records at the local level allows their immediate use and analysis to meet particular needs.

Supervision is more effective if it is not exercised from a distance by managers or commanders known only by name. Quotas for individual recruiters are more likely to be realistic and attainable if they are based on local experience and deci-sion, rather than formulated at a headquarters outside the region. The practices of individual recruiters can be closely monitored locally to make sure that established requirements and guide-lines are not compromised to meet quotas.

Military recruiting has long since become more than obtain-ing the required numbers of people with enough education and aptitude to serve successfully in one of the military services with little additional training. With military equipment, weap-ons systems, communications, and tactics becoming more and more technically complex, a wide range of general capabilities and special skills is needed. Military operations cannot be organized into a set of standardized actions which can be conducted by men and women with little comprehension of what is occurring beyond their immediate assignment.

The U.S. Army is a specific example of the organization of military recruiting. Its 2,500 recruiters throughout the nation are obligated to meet the force requirements set by congressional funding and assignment by army headquarters. The army enlists one-half of the total recruits entering the armed services. To this end, the country is divided into five regions called brigades in military terminology, each divided into smaller regions or battalions which in turn are subdivided into still smaller areas termed companies. It is at this last level that quotas are assigned to individual recruiters operating out of cities where the company stations are located.

Figure 46 on page 131 shows the total territory covered by the sixth (western) recruiting brigade, with headquarters at San Francisco, and the area covered by each of its eight battalions and their headquarters. The further spatial subdivision into smaller companies and centers is not shown.

The size and shape of the territory covered by each of the eight battalion regions are determined by population density, geographical considerations relating to easy access, the area of influence of one or two major cities in the region, and finally adjustment of the battalion borders to coincide with county boundaries. For administrative convenience the borders of the smallest recruiting areas also coincide with county boundaries, and their size relates to the feasible travel distance for a recruiter operating out of a centrally located community.

In its organizational division into regions, subregions, and smaller marketing areas, and in its assignment of quotas, army recruitment is not unlike the organization of some business operations for the sale of a product or service and the assignment of quotas for each sales person.

construction projects   During the 212 years since it was established to conduct mining and sapping operations for the Continental Army of the United States, the U.S. Army Corps of Engineers has expanded to include many and varied civil and military endeavors.

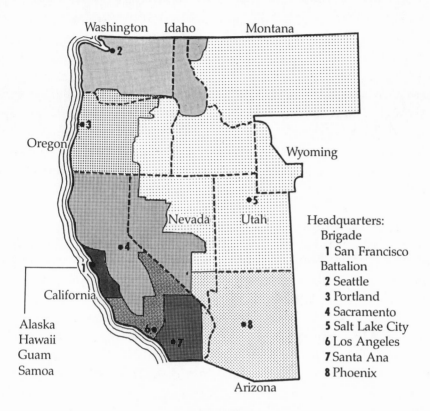

Figure 46
RECRUITMENT: U.S. ARMY
Interstate
Military Command, Administration
Operational
References: Program & Analysis Division, *Evaluation Directorate*, United
States Army Recruiting Command, Fort Sheridan, IL, 1 January 1986.
Fred O'Donnell, Chief, Advertising and Sales Promotion, U.S. Army
Recruiting Battalion, Los Angeles, CA, Personal Communication,
22 March 1987.

In time of war it ceases immediately those of its civil activities that are not directly connected with the war effort and functions as a combat support unit within the U.S. Army. In World War II one out of every six persons in the army was in the corps of engineers. Even brief indication of the range of engineering operations undertaken by the corps in wartime requires more space than is available here. In peacetime the corps engages in civil and military construction, regulatory activities, and research.

A major responsibility is maintaining and improving the navigability of the 25,000 miles of inland and coastal waterways that constitute a vital surface transportation system within the nation. The task includes dredging more than 350 million cubic yards of material every year, stabilizing hundreds of miles of river and stream banks, and operating some 220 primary facilities and 170 major dams built mainly to improve navigation. By 1987, 100 projects were generating more than 20 million kilowatts of electricity, a substantial percentage of the hydroelectric power produced in the United States.

For the past 50 years, three officers of the corps have served on the Mississippi River Commission as it gradually acquired authority to decide which levees, floodways, spillways, reservoirs, and other waterworks should be built and maintained with the money appropriated by Congress for the huge drainage basin of the Mississippi River and its tributaries covering one-half of the continental United States. The 300 to 400 dams that have been built primarily for flood control in this vast basin suggest the scale of this never ending effort.

In connection with both of the above assignments, the corps issues the permits that are required for any person, firm, or agency—including federal, state, and local governments—planning to perform work in the waterways and wetlands of the nation. This includes dredging, construction of piers, wharves, bulkheads, revetments, and breakwaters, rip rap and road fills, and the installation of wires, cables, and pipelines. Severe penalties can be imposed for failure to conform.

In addition to the extensive construction involved in maintaining the navigability of the nation's waterways, the corps has completed many large civil and military projects ranging from several of the biggest centers of the National Aeronautics and Space Administration (NASA) to launch sites and related facilities for the intercontinental ballistic missile system. Much construction also takes place abroad at the many installations operated by U.S. military services around the world.

In recent years, partly in response to criticism directed at some of its projects, the corps of engineers has broadened its study of their environmental effects. Also, since the passage of environmental legislation in the early 1970s, the corps is now concerned with water quality and waste disposal. It maintains five research laboratories engaged in waterways experiments, engineering and topographic investigations, cold regions research and engineering, water resource support, and construction and engineering.

Since its beginning, the corps of engineers has recognized the desirabilty of spatial and organizational decentralization. This has become a necessity as the corps has become the world's largest construction agency, employing around 40,000 people on the average, 1,000 of whom are military personnel.

> The Corps is divided into eleven (11) divisions which are subdivided into a total of thirty-six (36) districts nationwide. The decentralized nature of the Corps insures quick response and assistance to any area in the event of disaster. (Bratton, 1982)

Each of the 11 continental divisions—or regions as defined in this book—is commanded by a flag officer, with two deputies, one for civil and one for military activities. As shown in Figure 47 on page 134, divisions are delineated by the ridge line between major drainage basins. This topographical subdivision of the country relates to the corp's responsibility for the waterways and drainage systems of the continental United States.

In addition to the 36 districts in the United States, there is one in Japan and one in Korea. Like the divisions, the districts have dual deputies, except where there is no military or no civil construction in the district. Like the division boundaries, district borders are aligned with drainage areas rather than governmental jurisdictions.

In wartime, units of the corps of engineers are attached to theater, area, or regional military commands.

Alaska

North Pacific

Missouri River

North Central

New England

North Atlantic

South Pacific

Ohio River

Pacific Ocean
Division: Hawaii

Southwestern

South Atlantic

Virgin
Islands

Lower
Mississippi
Valley

• Division [Regional] Headquarters
⊛ Division and District Headquarters
  (Districts not shown)

▬ Regional boundaries are lines dividing drainage basins.

Figure 47
PROJECTS: U.S. ARMY CORPS OF ENGINEERS
Intranational
Military Services, Civil Government
Operational
Reference: *The United States Directory of Federal Regional Structure, 1981–1982,*
Washington, DC (The National Archives of the United States), p. 53.

operations   The United States Coast Guard is a unique and complex
organization which serves the diverse roles of military service, regulator, operator, ambassador, and handyman . . .
an establishment of about 38,300 military men and women
and 5,600 civilians . . . augmented by 12,000 reservists and
over 40,000 civilian volunteer auxiliaries. (U.S. Department of Transportation, United States Coast Guard, 1986)

Its activities are decentralized. Two area commands direct,
support, and coordinate the actions of districts, which are the
regional organizations performing the actual operations in the
field, in direct contact with those affected by coast guard activities. Atlantic area command supports seven districts, Pacific
area command five. Figure 48 on page 135 shows the area covered by the 11th district with regional headquarters at Long
Beach, California. This is the largest coast guard district,

involving almost 3,000 military personnel, some 500 civilian employees, 40 vessels of various types and sizes, and 13 airplanes and helicopters.

The operational authority of each district commander, a rear admiral, requires coordination of the different but interrelated activities conducted within the district, in accordance with plans, directives, and funding determined at coast guard headquarters. Regional activities include military preparedness and operations, maritime search and rescue, commercial vessel and recreational boating safety, enforcement of laws and treaties, aids to navigation, port and environmental safety, bridge administration, waterways management, marine environment response, international affairs, and ice operations.

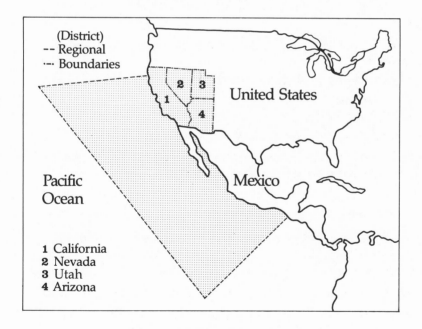

Figure 48
OPERATIONS: U.S. COAST GUARD
Intranational, Interstate, International
Military Services, Civil Government
Operational
Reference: Department of Transportation, United States Coast Guard,
Organization Manual (COMDTINST M5400.7B), Washington, D.C., 1986,
p. 1.1.1.

Although the United States Coast Guard is part of the Department of Transportation rather than the Department of Defense, it is gradually being given military responsibility for the coastal defense of the nation in addition to its other activities.

Besides its operations along the seacoast, within the land portion of the 11th district there are recruiting offices, navigational direction and other facilities located away from the coast, and coast guard vessels performing those of its seagoing operations appropriate for several inland navigable river systems. Each district also conducts the particular planning, logistic, legal, and administrative support required to carry out any single or combined operation.

Each district commander is directing a subsystem which is part of the total system planned and controlled at coast guard headquarters in Washington, DC. Within the region he coordinates and plans comprehensively the different activities he directs.

Business

oil and gas exploration and development

Oil and gas exploration and production are necessarily associated with the regions on earth where geological and botanical conditions occurring eons ago created this subterranean resource essential to industrial society. As known reserves are exhausted, the search for new supplies continues—onshore, from platforms operating farther and farther offshore, in the icy Artic, tropical jungles, wherever around the world exploratory surveys are promising.

> ARCO International Oil and Gas Company . . . is aggressively developing a number of recent discoveries that will expand overseas production. . . . The Company acquired new exploration acreage in Ireland, Italy, and Turkey and is currently negotiating for exploration licenses in Pakistan and Denmark. ARCO is also pursuing new exploration opportunities offshore China and Norway. (Atlantic Richfield Company, 1985)

Figure 49 on page 137 shows the regions of the world outside the continental United States and Alaska where ARCO is producing and exploring for oil and natural gas. These functional activities of the ARCO International Oil and Gas Company are regional in two ways. Geographically, underground hydrocarbon deposits are found only in certain regions where particular subsurface geological conditions exist. Administratively, Arco has decentralized its global exploration and production outside the United States by establishing eight subsidiary companies which manage these activities in nodal regions located in or around Indonesia, Greenland, Britain, Norway, Dubai, China, Turkey, and the Suez.

The North American Electic Reliability Council (NERC) is a *electric* voluntary organization supported by its membership, consist- *reliability* ing of nine regional councils coordinating the activities of 332 participating electric utility systems throughout the United States and Canada. It came into being as part of the aftermath of the 1965 blackout in the northeastern United States. (Figure 50, North American Electric Reliability Council, page 138)

That occurrence convinced industry and government leaders that the rapidly developing systems of interconnected

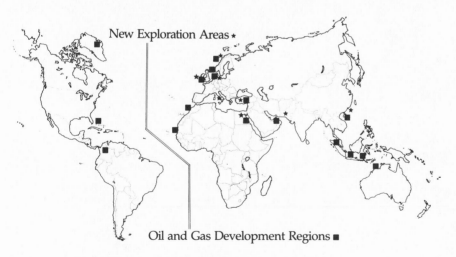

Figure 49
OIL AND GAS EXPLORATION AND DEVELOPMENT:
ATLANTIC RICHFIELD COMPANY
Global
Business Administration, Geology, Engineering
Operations
Reference: Atlantic Richfield Company, *1985 Supplement to the Annual Report*,
Los Angeles, CA, p. 27.

Figure 50
**ELECTRIC RELIABILITY: NORTH AMERICAN ELECTRIC RELIABILITY
COUNCIL**
International
Engineering, Business, Civil Government
Operations
Reference: North American Electric Reliability Council, *Annual Report 1984*,
Princeton, NJ, 1984, Back Front Cover, opposite p. 1.

utilities would require additional coordination to reestab-
lish reliability and to prevent such widespread blackouts
from occurring again (NERC, 1984).

Technical requirements and the public necessity of providing uninterrupted electric energy to more than 270 million people and hundreds of thousands of productive activities of many
kinds makes coordination a practical necessity rather than a
choice. There is always the possibility of federally mandated
requirements if voluntary coordination fails.

The central staff of NERC supports the regional councils
and their operating and engineering committees and subcommittees, and maintains the Power Line Carrier Data Base, the

General Availability Data System, and the Interregional Emergency Network.

The operating committee, consisting of two to four representatives from each of the nine regional councils, maintains a manual of recommendations and guidelines for the reliable performance of the interconnected power system. Six subcommittees recommend methods and procedures for the following activities: responsive system control, monitoring conformance to operating guides; improved reliability and bulk power generation and transmission during emergencies; information transfer between individual utility systems and between regions; monitoring performance of the unified control of interconnected power systems; annual review of disturbances that occur in the bulk power system; and on-site review and confidential critique of utility control centers.

The activities of the engineering committee, with two members from each regional council, are also best described by those of its subcommittees: annual review of the reliability of electric energy in North America for the next 10 years; reliability concepts in bulk power electric systems; annual computer models of the existing and planned bulk power system, including generators, transmission lines, and loads; and studies of the effects on electric power systems of operations or events in space that generate electromagnetic pulses which can disrupt sensitive equipment on the ground.

These various activities represent functional planning and operating coordination in close combination.

"Since its inception 16 years ago, [North American Reliability] Council has aimed its unique resources at a single target—a reliable supply of electricity now and for the future." (NERC, 1984)

This requires accurate forecasting of future demand for electricity because it takes years to design and construct new power generation and distribution facilities. This has proved to be a difficult task. For 35 years prior to 1974 the use of electricity in the United States increased about seven percent per year. This growth rate decreased by two-thirds during the following ten years, with an actual decline in the use of electricity in 1982.

Since then growth has resumed at twice the low rate predicted by the utilities.

> Electricity use and economic activity still seem to be inextricably linked. . . . Because electricity use is a function of so many forces outside the control of utilities, such as the economy and the weather, forecasts of future electricity requirements cannot be any more certain than the forecasts of these many external factors. (NERC, 1984)

Existing and planned facilities and systems must be analyzed continually to ensure that market demand for electricity in the future is met and the possibility of interrupted service or blackout is minimized. To accomplish this certain data bases must be maintained and up-to-the-minute information provided among the several hundred participating utilities interconnected within and between regions into a network covering the entire United States and most of Canada. Operations must be monitored continuously.

Regional concepts are fundamental to the entire endeavor. Electric power distribution systems are most efficient if they are not spatially confined to a politically defined governmental jurisidiction but conform to the most efficient regional size and arrangement of the power distribution system itself. The regional concept is basic to the organization of the different power producing entities into interconnected systems supporting each other in times of exceptional demand and unusual or emergency situations of various kinds.

> As never before, system operators need effective and far-reaching interregional coordination to maintain established standards of reliability. Economic incentives have created the impetus for daily transfers of energy across geographically-wide transmission interfaces; these power exchanges test the capacity of the transmission system and its operations. To achieve the degree of coordination among regions needed under these conditions, system operators must be better versed in regional matters, making excellent communications paramount. (NERC, 1984)

Because functional planning has to do with a single concern, activity, or operational element does not mean that it is simpler than subsystem planning or comprehensive planning by a higher level of management in a different application of the planning process. The activities of the Electric Reliability Council illustrate the scope and complexity of functional planning which involves complex activities and is itself conducted comprehensively, taking into account all of the critical elements that must be considered for successful operations.

Many companies find that they cannot effectively manage *sales* their business activities throughout the United States from a single national headquarters. Operations are conducted more successfully when they are decentralized, with regional executives responsible for management within their area of responsibility. They can maintain closer contact with the market for the product or service, with the operating personnel of the company in the field, and with the many organizations involved in their activities. Figure 33 on page 70 provides a sampling of the number and diversity of such regional operations. Figure 34 on page 71 illustrates a specific example:

Most sales activities are decentralized with regional *automotive* managers for such activities as retail sales, parts sales, fleet *manufacturers* sales, used truck sales, finance and administration and service located at the regional headquarters.

Coordination is provided by means of a reporting relationship to the Vice President-Sales located at corporate headquarters in Chicago. Reporting to [this individual] are various staff positions that provide services to the various regions . . . systems development, sales program development, sales training, advertising, and other support.

The performance of the regions is monitored and measured at corporate headquarters.

Most marketing activities are centralized . . . market research, market planning, product development, forecasting, competitive research and pricing. With the exception of forecasting and pricing, most marketing activities are conducted without regard to regional considerations. Any such corporate analysis is then communicated to the corporate sales group for regional applications. (Personal Communication, 1986)

greeting   Greeting cards are a very different product than automotive
  cards   manufactures, but the advantages of managerial decentraliza-
          tion apply to most products and most business organizations.
          Advertising and sales of a leading greeting card company are
          directed regionally. The content and design of the cards varies
          for different parts of the country and sometimes between smaller
          territories or districts within regions. For instance, cards sold
          in the U.S. Southwest have a greater ethnic content than in
          other sections of the nation, reflecting differences in the com-
          position of their populations. The scenery depicted on cards
          varies according to the physical characteristics of sales areas;
          desert scenes are not found on greeting cards sold in the state
          of Maine. On the other hand, there is little difference between
          the message or other communicative content of cards sold in
          different regions.

          Other things being equal, production plants, warehouses,
          and distribution centers are situated geographically with respect
          to each other and potential markets so that the time and cost
          of distributing cards to the leased or licensed outlets is
          minimized.

          Computers show graphically the location of all outlets as
          they relate to markets and to each other. The number and type
          of cards in each "slot" in the outlet display are monitored reg-
          ularly, recording the sales of each type of card. This form of
          "point-of-sale" recording permits periodical tabulation of the
          profitability of each greeting card by outlet, district, and region.
          It also provides an up-to-the-minute accounting of inventory
          and production needs.

          Regional management of selected functions is employed by
          companies engaged in business abroad. Usually a regional level
          of management covering a continent, a number of countries,
          a nation, or even a locality is required because of the significant
          differences between the ethnology and demography of popu-
          lations around the world: their language, culture and customs,
          composition, needs and desires, attitudes and behavior. Nor-
          mally it is impossible for a global headquarters staff to regularly
          collect, absorb, and integrate this diverse informational input,
          make sound business decisions for operations in different parts
          of the world, and see that they are effectively carried out.

Timely production and distribution of the national edition *production*
of *The Wall Street Journal* five days a week for 2 million sub- *distribution*
scribers located throughout the United States is a noteworthy *sales*
operational achievement requiring regional organization.

The Journal's editorial headquarters in New York city selects,
edits, and processes the day's most important business news
and information. This is transmitted from New York to the four
regions shown in Figure 51 on page 143 by a satellite in sta-
tionary orbit over the Galapagos Islands in the Pacific Ocean
off the northwest coast of South America to five regional composing centers: at Chicopee and Orlando in the east, Naperville
in the midwest, Dallas in the southwest, and Palo Alto in the

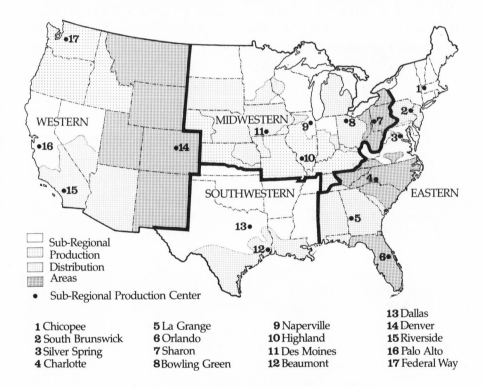

☐ Sub-Regional
▦ Production
▦ Distribution
▦ Areas

● Sub-Regional Production Center

			13 Dallas
1 Chicopee	**5** La Grange	**9** Naperville	**14** Denver
2 South Brunswick	**6** Orlando	**10** Highland	**15** Riverside
3 Silver Spring	**7** Sharon	**11** Des Moines	**16** Palo Alto
4 Charlotte	**8** Bowling Green	**12** Beaumont	**17** Federal Way

Figure 51
PRODUCTION, DISTRIBUTION, SALES:
THE WALL STREET JOURNAL
Intranational
Business Management
Operations
Reference: *The Wall Street Journal*, 24 January 1983, p. 16.

west. Part of the news sent to these centers has been selected
or tailored for regional editions. Dow Jones & Company which
publishes the Journal was the first private enterprise in the
United States licensed to own and operate a transmitting and
receiving earth station.

Material prepared at the five composing centers is retrans-
mitted by satellite to receiving stations in each of the four regions.
Here, local information is added. For example, at Palo Alto in
the western region, local advertising and other regional content are added to the material received from the composing
centers. The final press-ready plates resulting from this combination of materials are reprinted in the Palo Alto plant for
distribution within its service area, and are transmitted elec-
tronically to Riverside in California, Federal Way in Washington
state, and Denver in Colorado for printing and distribution
within these subdivisions of the western region. The newspaper is produced in its final form in the same way for the
other three regional editions.

Two editions of the Journal are printed, one for distribution
to the outlying portions of the service area, a second several
hours later for readers closer by containing late news items just
received. The papers are delivered by bulk sales, carrier services to individual addresses, or to post offices.

This complex and technologically sophisticated subsystem
of Dow Jones for producing a newspaper—involving the collection and dissemination of news and other information,
advertising, electronic communication, managerial organization, printing, sales, and distribution—can only be outlined
briefly in the space available here. But it is clear that regional
organization at several levels is an essential part of such an
operation extending to every corner of the continental United
States, to Hawaii and Alaska, parts of Mexico and Canada, and
several of the islands in the Caribbean. In a similar manner,
the European and Asiatic editions of the Journal are produced
in Heerlen in The Netherlands and Hong Kong, and distributed from these centers throughout the nodal regions they
serve.

energy   As the largest energy producing public utility in the United
States, Pacific Gas & Electric Company (PG&E) supplies elec-

tricity to nearly 3.8 million customers and natural gas to more than 3 million people. Its service area in California, shown in Figure 52 on page 145, covers 94,000 square miles: an area larger than 42 of the 50 states. The installations and facilities required to service this large territory represent an investment of approximately $16.5 billion. PG&E employs some 28,000 people.

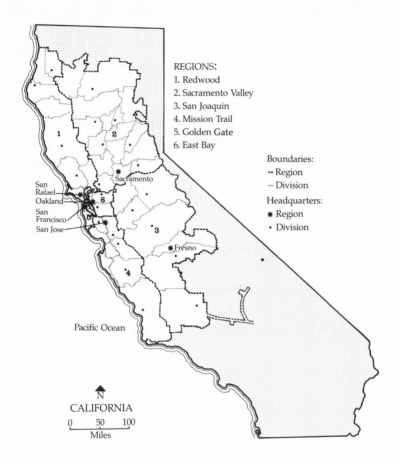

REGIONS:
1. Redwood
2. Sacramento Valley
3. San Joaquin
4. Mission Trail
5. Golden Gate
6. East Bay

Boundaries:
-- Region
-- Division

Headquarters:
* Region
• Division

Pacific Ocean

N
CALIFORNIA
0   50   100
Miles

Figure 52
PRODUCTION, DISTRIBUTION, SALES:
PACIFIC GAS & ELECTRIC COMPANY
Intrastate
Engineering, Business Administration
Operational
Reference: Kaderali, Shiraz R., Director of Special Projects, Planning and Research, Pacific Gas & Electric Company, San Francisco, CA, Personal Communication, March 1987.

For the company to function efficiently and provide prompt response to the diverse needs of its many customers, PG&E has decentralized its distributive organization into regions and divisions. The size of these subdivisions is determined by the number of customers served, the total demand for energy within the area, and geographical considerations.

The boundaries of these two spatial categories shown in Figure 52 coincide only occasionally with county borders, which are not included in the figure because their addition would produce a tangle of lines difficult to decipher. Without exception the PG&E subdivisions of the state for its purposes do not coincide exactly with the jurisdictional areas of counties. Some of them, however, may extend close by on either side or alternately on both sides of a governmental boundary. This statewide discrepancy between governmental jurisdictions and utility divisions reflects the historical derivation of the one and the operational designation of the other. Statistics conforming to a county's governmental jurisdiction, accumulated over years to indicate trends, must be adjusted to relate the data to the PG&E operational subdivisions.

The 28 divisions of the company are the primary interface between PG&E and its customers. In both administrative and military terminology they are "line" units performing directive or "command" functions in the field. These operational activities include maintaining and extending the electric and natural gas distribution systems within their area, marketing and sales promotion, customer services, land management, building maintenance, materials supply, and personnel administration and recruitment. These line activities are carried out in accordance with general corporate policies, objectives, and directives.

> The company is in the midst of implementing some major changes to allow greater decision making authority at the division and regional levels. The concept is to ultimately be able to measure the performance of each unit on a revenue and cost basis. As such, the objective is to make each unit relatively independent. (Kaderali, 1987)

The six regions act as supportive "staff" to the divisions and as intermediaries between them and corporate headquarters. They are responsible for substations and load centers supplying the energy subsystems operated by the divisions. The regional units conduct those aspects of marketing, energy management, conservation, building administration, and bulk purchasing which must be or are best handled at a regional scale. They also maintain records of the collective performance of the divisions within each region.

Pacific Gas & Electric Company is an excellent example of a large private enterprise, serving many people throughout a large area, which finds it most efficient to decentralize as many as possible of its operations and management decisions to the local level where direct and daily contact with customers can be maintained, and operational efficiency is best evaluated.

After serving as political advisor to Franklin D. Roosevelt during his unprecedented four terms as President of the United States, James A. Farley made a surprising if not startling statement in his subsequent position as chairman of the board of directors of The Coca-Cola Company. He announced the company was embarking on a program to produce and sell Coca-Cola around the world. *soft drink*

The announcement was received with considerable skepticism. At the time, Coca-Cola was almost exclusively an American soft drink, as indigenous as apple pie or popcorn. The idea of a soft drink company competing abroad with the beers, wines, and other native beverages of foreign countries around the world seemed presumptuous. Most people thought money spent in the effort would end up a total loss.

In the intervening years Coca-Cola has proven these skeptics entirely wrong. It successfully promoted and produced its product globally well before the recent explosive expansion in international trade brought about by national differences in labor costs, improved transportation and communication systems, technology transfer, and greater industrialization of developing countries. Whereas at one time the foot-driven Singer sewing machine was the product of the industrialized western world most likely to be found in the market square of a native village, it has long since been replaced by an ancient Coca-Cola sign above a doorway and several empty cases stacked outside. Coca-Cola is the most ubiquitous international trademark found around the world today.

Coca-Cola's foreign operations are decentralized just short of completely independent subsidiaries. The parent corporation in Atlanta, Georgia, does not produce products. It acts as a giant staff providing market services developed over many years of successful experience to hundreds of independent bottlers in the United States and abroad. It makes recommendations on various matters: ways of strengthening and expanding trademark identification and favorable consumer response to Coca-Cola; maintaining a public preference for Coca-Cola products over the competition; introducing new soft drinks; and making the most of material supply situations or production opportunities that could be employed profitably by producers in different parts of the world. Corporate headquarters staff serves the producing units as management consultants rather than as "line" officials giving orders.

Coca-Cola divides international operations organizationally into three continental regions: Latin America, Europe-Africa, and Pacific. A group vice president located at the company's headquarters in Atlanta channels corporate staff services to those divisions marketing Coca-Cola products within his continental region. He makes policy, monitors performance, reviews division plans, provides strategic direction, and generally acts as consultative liaison between the parent corporation and the divisional operating units.

Each division is responsible for marketing, production, and sales of Coca-Cola through its independent bottler system within a specified area or region. The chief executive officer of the division is responsible for all aspects of its operations: manufacturing, production, purchasing, personnel, finance, sales, distribution, advertising, public relations, and other related activities within the region. Every year each division prepares a three-year projection and plan indicating what its chief executive officer expects and commits himself to accomplish during the forthcoming three years. The plan is reviewed by the group vice president in the United States and other senior corporate managers. However, the division manager is subject only to certain general corporate policies, recommendations concerning marketing, advice concerning global opportunities which can benefit his operations, and achievement of the specific objectives stated in the plan.

The Coca-Cola Company exemplifies several applications of the regional concept and the planning process. There is an organizational distinction between domestic and foreign operations, two very large regions of activity. Foreign operations in turn are divided into three continental regions for managerial overview and support. Each of these supports a number of divisions responsible for Coca-Cola's operations within smaller regions. The divisions engage in comprehensive planning since they generally conduct all aspects of their operations, subject only to certain established corporate policies, product specifications, and supportive recommendations. The group vice presidents engage in a limited form of regional planning: providing strategic direction and certain supportive services, and making sure that the continental regions grow and remain profitable.

Civil Government

The control of locusts and grasshoppers presents a very difficult problem of regional planning in certain parts of the world involving continents, winds, precipitation, pesticides, and the complex breeding and behavior of the four species of locusts—not to mention the technical, financial, and cooperative capabilities of the nations, governmental agencies, and international organizations concerned. *pest control*

A locust eats its own weight every day. A swarm may number a billion insects and 100 swarms may be on the move during a plague, covering 200 miles a day while moving 2,000 miles. An invasion can destroy all crops in its path with disastrous economic and social consequences in the region affected.

For the first time in 40 years, grasshoppers and all four species of locusts active in Africa are posing a serious threat simultaneously. In all, a score of countries in Africa are menaced. (Figure 53, page 150)

A major question is whether to help rebuild and maintain an effective antilocust control and research capability in the region. . . . Does the cost of maintaining an effective control organization outweigh the risks of being unprepared for the next serious outbreak? (Walsh, 1986)

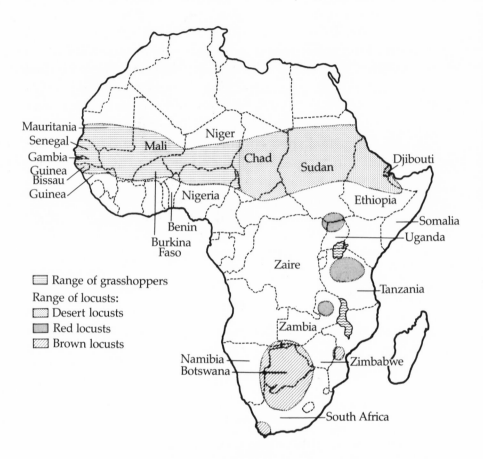

Figure 53
PEST CONTROL: LOCUSTS AND GRASSHOPPERS
Intranational
Entomology, Agricultural Science
Descriptive
Intermittent
Reference: Walsh, John, "Return of the Locust: A Cloud Over Africa,"
Science, 3 October 1986, p. 19.

A threatened plague of grasshoppers and locusts has been brought under control in much of western and eastern Africa. . . .

Southern Africa, however, remains "a danger zone." . . . Botswana is preparing to face a second year of plague . . . Angola, Lesotho, Namibia, Mozambique, Swaziland and Zimbabwe could all be invaded if control efforts now underway fail. (*The New York Times*, 1986)

The problems presented by locusts, grasshoppers, Mediterranean fruit flies, South American "killer" bees, Asian flying cockroaches, and other destructive insects are recognized. As more and more people and products are transported between various parts of the world, the containment of pests and diseases becomes correspondingly more difficult, if not impossible.

Since insects and infectious organisms do not respect jurisdictional boundaries, regional planning organizationally related to the area of infestation or infection is required to eradicate contamination or prevent its spread to other countries or continents. The Onchocerciasis (River Blindness) Control Program illustrated by Figure 22 on page 48 is an example. If inadvertent contamination cannot be eradicated or contained within a single jurisdiction, regional planning must be expanded to cover the area of actual and potential infestation.

Although the U.S. Internal Revenue Service collects and processes over 180 million tax returns and more than 750 billion dollars every year, it is a single functional activity of the federal government. With an annual budget of over $4 billion and 100,000 employees, operational decentralization is clearly necessary. No activity of such magnitude involving the entire population and every corner of a large and populous nation could be conducted by a central staff from a single national headquarters. *revenue collection*

The three levels of the bureau's organization are reflected in Figure 43 on page 93: a national office, regional offices, and district offices. Directly under the office of the commissioner and deputy commissioner of internal revenue in Washington, DC is a large national office. Operations, policy and management, and data processing are each headed by an associate commissioner. All aspects of tax affairs are conducted, policies determined, and directives issued by the national office to the field offices in seven regions.

Within these regional offices, regional commissioners administer the activities of a total of 63 districts and 10 strategically located service centers. There are also regional inspectors and regional counsels with their staffs at each of the seven field offices. Legal counsels are also located at most of the district offices.

The basic operations performed by the Service include resources management, collection, examination and processing of tax returns, accounting, criminal investigation, litigation, audit, and security. There is a national computer center in West Virginia and a data center in Michigan. The location of the computer center in Appalachia probably relates to improving economic conditions in this depressed section of the nation, discussed later in this chapter as an example of regional economic development.

The Internal Revenue Service is a centralized organization. Regional and district offices do not act independently within a set of objectives and general guidelines, but effectuate policies, requirements, and procedures determined in the nation's capitol. Because local conditions vary among different parts of the country, field offices do have considerable latitude in how they carry out directives from above. Only to this limited extent is the IRS administratively decentralized. This contrasts with the administrative organization of the U.S. Coast Guard and The Coca-Cola Company discussed on pages 147–149.

water The Metropolitan Water District of Southern California
supply (MWD) was created in 1928 as a regional public agency to provide water to the Los Angeles area. Today this area has expanded enormously to cover more than 5,000 square miles extending along the coast of California for 200 miles to the Mexican border and inland from the sea some 75 miles. Thirteen million people live within this service district which includes portions of 6 counties and 135 cities. (Figure 54, page 153)

The District has an investment of more than $1.5 billion in facilities which include a 242-mile aqueduct from the

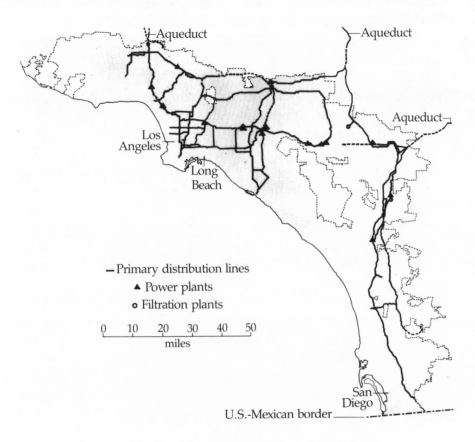

Figure 54
**WATER SUPPLY: METROPOLITAN WATER DISTRICT
OF SOUTHERN CALIFORNIA**
Intrastate, Intercounty, Special District
Civil Government, Civil Engineering
Operations
Reference: Landsman, S. H. (Compiler and Editor), *Annual Report for the
Fiscal Year, July 1, 1984 to June 30, 1985*, The Metropolitan Water District of
Southern California, Los Angeles, CA, p. 7 (Figure 2).

Colorado River . . . 5 pumping plants, 700 miles of large
diameter distribution pipelines, 5 water treatment plants,
12 reservoirs, a series of hydroelectric power plants, and
numerous support facilities. . . .

[It] has authority to levy taxes on property within its
boundaries, to establish water rates, to sell bonds for construction projects, to acquire property through the power
of eminent domain, and to sell water for other beneficial
uses. (The Metropolitan Water District of Southern California, 1984)

The MWD is an example of a special district established as
a regional agency to perform a single function, in this case
supplying a water short area with imported water. Local supplies could not support the tremendous growth that has occurred
in coastal southern California during the past 50 years. The
many separate governmental units within the service area cannot possibly meet the demands of the present population from
underground aquifers or streams within their jurisdiction. They
cannot individually procure or exercise rights to water from a
distant source. Nor can they separately finance the purchase
of necessary rights-of-way and the large capital expenditures
required to construct facilities to import water over considerable distances. For these reasons a regional agency was essential.

The district does not supply all of the water needed within
its service area. Normally, the city of Los Angeles, which has
an extensive system of its own bringing water from over 300
miles away, purchases only 5 percent of what it needs from the
MWD. During dry years when precipitation is below normal
in headwater areas, Los Angeles may require triple the amount
usually purchased. Most cities in the district are dependent on
it for all or nearly all of their supply.

The MWD must engage in extensive planning to preserve
the existing system and meet urban water demand which is
expected to increase by between 24 and 36 percent by the end
of the century. New sources of supply, water conservation, and
recycling are being investigated. New facilities must be designed,
engineered and specified in detail. The existing system must
be maintained in optimum working order, including minimiz-
ing possible interruption of service by earthquakes in high risk

southern California. At the request of its member agencies, the district has prepared a regional urban water management plan evaluating "past and present water conservation and managerial activities to be implemented in the future." Also, "A major study was begun to determine . . . the scope and magnitude of the groundwater quality problem and its impact, if any, on the continued availability of local water supplies" (Landsman, 1985). Environmental procedures of the district reflect changes in state and federal environmental legislation.

An integral part of planning comprehensively for this functional activity involves forecasts of water and hydroelectric power sales; income from levies based on real property assessments and other sources; operating, depreciation, amortization, and interest expense; and cash flow. Also required for successful planning are effective corporate organization and staff support, sound managment policies, and efficient internal administration.

This special district illustrates the managerial complications created when many governmental units are combined in one regional organization. The MWD includes 135 representatives from the cities served, 51 members on its board of directors and between 16 and 18 members on each of its 7 standing committees. Undoubtedly, this broad representation and directorial participation are considered necessary to protect the interests of each governmental jurisdiction served by the district. The policy-making and managerial difficulties to be expected among such a large number of decision makers are more likely to be resolved when the regional activity is a single function performed by a special district established for this single purpose. Much depends on the capabilities of the general manager and nine divisional or departmental managers and their staffs who direct the planning and operations of the district.

In comprehensive planning the self-interest of the many participants involves the full range of civil governmental activities and concerns, each of which is subject to disagreement which can delay or prevent progress. The broader range of consideration increases the likelihood that there will be a deadlock on one or several of the key elements of comprehensive planning. Some of the new concerns introduced by the broader scope will by their nature be more controversial: such as the allocation of available funds among competing demands; provisions for protecting public health, persons, and property; low-income housing; treatment of the homeless; or minority representation. Most people agree that single governmental functions such as water supply, fire protection, or sewerage systems are essential. But the multiple elements covered in comprehensive planning may each be challenged for many reasons: relative importance, underlying policies, general treatment, funding, politics, special interests, external events, or methods of implementation.

development   From the beginning of the millenium the ancient Kingdom
project of Lanka on the island of Sri Lanka off the southeast coast of India fed its population and exported enough rice to be called the granary of the East. Ruins remain of the ancient water storage and irrigation system which made this possible.

By 1300 AD the Kingdom of Lanka had succumbed to invasion, civil strife, and a major malaria epidemic. During subsequent centuries the island was ruled by Sinhalese kings, Indian princes, China for half a century, the Portuguese, Dutch, and finally as Ceylon by the British.

For the last 100 years Sri Lanka has imported most of its food. Early irrigation systems were destroyed long ago. Three-quarters of the total area of the country (25,000 square miles) was a parched plain producing at best one crop of rice each year. Most of the population of 15 million were farmers cultivating the remaining one-quarter of the country, a rainy and fertile region producing two harvests per year.

By 1973 during the worldwide oil crisis, 25 years after Sri Lanka attained independence, the nation was spending most of its national income to import food and energy. Part of its population was queuing up for food. The government decided the country would have to become agriculturally self-sufficient. This required impounding and diverting some of the waters from that portion of the Mahaveli River located in the rainy region to irrigate one million acres of the parched portion of the land downstream, making it far more productive agriculturally.

The Mahaveli development project is a large system involving four large dams, reservoirs requiring the relocation of 43,000 homes located on the land to be inundated, major canals, tributary waterways, and small channels distributing the life-giving water to the properties of the 150,000 families resettled in the dry region. Each family is allotted three acres: two and one-half acres for cultivation, one-half acre for the homestead. (Figure 55, page 158)

As originally planned the total cost was projected to be $1.5 billion, with construction and relocation to be completed in 30 years. A new national government installed in 1977 decided to build the major portion of the project in 6 years. Sweden, Germany, Britain, Kuwait, Japan, and the United States assisted in this mammoth undertaking in different ways. The World Bank, the Asian Development Bank, and the United Nations participated in financing the project. By 1984, two dams were completed and the other two were under construction. An ancient reservoir was enlarged to cover 7 square miles (18.1 square kilometers) and incorporated into the project system. Water was supplied to 250,000 of the 750,000 people to be relocated. System management continues, educating individual farmers how to divert water for their own use in irrigation without preempting water allotted to families further along the supply line. Conformance must be monitored and misuses corrected.

This remarkable undertaking by a geographically small developing country with ethnic problems exemplifies subsystem planning and effectuation: impounding water, installing an irrigation system, the hydroelectric generation of electric power, and the education and general supervision of farmers in modern farming practices. While the project is national in scope and significance, its purpose is regional, to provide a better balance between the agricultural productivity and industrial development potential of two climatically and topographically different sections of the country.

One-half of The Netherlands would be flooded twice daily were it not for the dunes, dikes, barriers, and other large structures that the nation has built over the centuries to protect and reclaim land from the sea to support and house an increasing population. The most recent of these mammoth enterprises is the Delta Project.

reclamation project

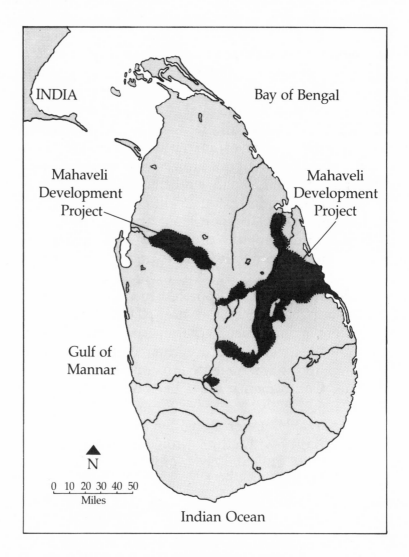

Figure 55
DEVELOPMENT PROJECT: SRI LANKA
Interregional
Civil Government, Engineering
Operations
Reference: Television Program, *Fountains of Paradise*, NOVA, WGBH
Educational Foundation, 1984.

> Continuously threatened by the tempestuous North Sea, the Dutch seek to protect the southern corner of their country with a colossal hydraulic-engineering project. Begun more than 30 years ago, after a savage North Sea storm devastated much of the southern Netherlands, the five-billion-dollar Delta Project . . . a vast complex of dams, dikes, and channels . . . will safeguard both a valuable estuarine environment and further generations of Dutch. (Kohl, 1986)

In recent years, the formulation of regional plans in Holland and their adoption by provincial councils has been discontinued. The areas covered by these plans did not coincide with the jurisdictional boundaries of the governmental unit or units which prepare or participate in the preparation of plans, implement them, or within whose territory they will be realized. These regional plans required a fourth level of integration. In a country the size of The Netherlands, three levels of planning and administration are now considered sufficient: national, provincial, and municipal. By contrast, in the United States Florida has recently introduced and mandated a fourth level of planning, discussed on page 169.

Not all regional plans have been discontinued. Certain large projects require cooperation among local government units. Also, a special authority must be established to plan and construct projects involving a territory that does not coincide with existing governmental boundaries. The Ijsselmeer Polders scheme to reclaim the Zuyder Zee, the Delta plan, and the Waddenzee project to reclaim large areas of land from the sea are examples of such regional development planning.

> These major multi-purpose projects are carried out by semi-autonomous regional development agencies under the auspices of the Department of Water Management [and Traffic] . . . unhindered by inter-departmental and pro-vincial-municipal conflicts . . . As the projects proceed, reclaimed land is returned to the control of adjacent provinces." (Glasson, 1978)

The Colorado River and its tributaries constitute a geographical region of primary importance to a substantial section *river basin development* of the nation (Figure 56, Development: Colorado River Basin, page 160).

Colorado River
system

The Colorado River drains practically the entire [southwest] corner of the continental United States . . . It is virtually the sole dependable water supply for an area of 244,000 square miles, including parts of seven states . . .

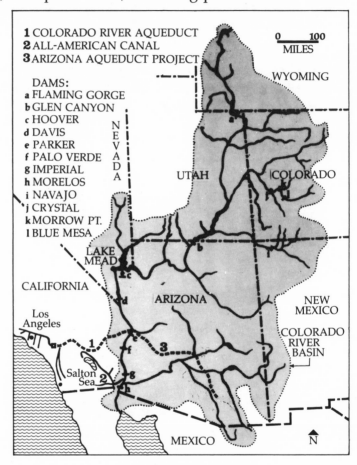

1 COLORADO RIVER AQUEDUCT
2 ALL-AMERICAN CANAL
3 ARIZONA AQUEDUCT PROJECT

DAMS:
a FLAMING GORGE
b GLEN CANYON
c HOOVER
d DAVIS
e PARKER
f PALO VERDE
g IMPERIAL
h MORELOS
i NAVAJO
j CRYSTAL
k MORROW PT.
l BLUE MESA

Figure 56
DEVELOPMENT: COLORADO RIVER BASIN
Interstate
Multi-Purpose, River Basin Planning
References: Hundley, Norris, Jr., *Water and the West*, The Colorado River Compact and the Politics of the Water in the American West, Berkeley, CA (University of California Press), 1975, 395 pp. Dennis B. Underwood, Executive Director, Colorado River Board of California, Los Angeles, CA, Personal Communication, 1987.

and Mexico. Its influence is also felt far beyond its own watershed, for its waters have been diverted hundreds of miles and used to stimulate growth of such areas as eastern Colorado, [central Arizona and New Mexico, central and western Utah, southern Nevada], and the coastal plain of southern California. . . . (Hundley, 1975)

In California alone, the Colorado River irrigates some 650,000 acres in the Imperial, Coachella, Palo Verde, and Yuma Valleys. It supplies municipal, industrial, and agricultural water and hydroelectric power to seven counties containing properties with over one-half of the state's total assessed valuation and over half of the state's population of 13 million people. The Metropolitan Water District of Southern California (Figure 54, page 153) is one of the six major public agencies with established water and power rights which have invested $800 million in facilities for the diversion and use of nearly 5 million acre-feet of water per year, and for the generation and transmission of 3.5 billion kilowatt-hours of hydroelectric power annually.

The Colorado River system is as important to metropolitan growth, numerous industries, agriculture, recreation, and scenic resources in the other six states as it is to southern California's explosive urban expansion. However, the relative importance of the different uses of water varies among the participating states and some of their needs are potential rather than immediate.

The allocation of its waters and the distribution of hydroelectric power generated at its dams represent three–quarters of a century of proposals, politics, advocacy, regional development, and prolonged litigation. In 1878 a western journalist urged federal action: "The disposition of its waters is a subject over which the General Government should assume entire control, devising some wise and comprehensive plan for irrigation works." In 1902, the future director of the U.S. Reclamation Service outlined for fellow engineers a general plan for "the gradual comprehensive development of the Colorado River by a series of large reservoirs." In 1922, the Colorado Compact was formalized "to provide for the equitable division and apportionment of the use of the waters of the Colorado River system; to establish the relative importance and beneficial uses of water; to promote interstate comity; to remove causes and effects of present and future controversies; and to secure the expeditious agricultural and industrial development of the Colorado River basin, the storage of its waters, and the protection of life and property from floods." These multiple purposes, together with the hydroelectric generation and distribution of power from the dams that have been built and the construction of large aqueducts, constitute multi-purpose regional planning.

> Measured by the vastness of the region and the magnitude of the interests regulated, the Colorado Compact represents, thus far [1925], the most ambitious illustration of interstate agreements. (Frankfurter and Landis, 1925)

> [It] marked the first time under the Constitution that a group of states apportioned the water of an interstate stream for consumption use and the first time that more than two or three states negotiated a treaty to settle any sort of problem among themselves. It established a precedent that other states soon initiated, though no subsequent water treaty involved as many states or dealt with an area as large, or a set of problems as complex, as those of the Colorado. It precipitated struggles that threw into sharp relief the interaction between the local and national levels, between state governments and the federal government, between private interests and public, between the East and the West, between the United States and Mexico. (Hundley, 1975)

The operation of the Colorado River reservoir system is a responsibility of the Secretary of the U.S. Department of the Interior in consultation with the seven river basin states, and in accordance with documents known collectively as "The Law of the River." These documents now include interstate compacts, federal legislation, water delivery contracts, state legislation, a treaty and other agreements with Mexico, U.S. Supreme Court decrees, and federal administrative actions.

In operating the reservoir facilities, the Secretary of the Interior must consider the uses of the reservoirs for all purposes including flood control, river regulation, beneficial consumptive use, power production, water quality control, recreation, enhancement of fish and wildlife, and other environmental factors. As shown in Figure 56 the river system involves 12 major storage and diversion dams, large aqueducts and canals, and numerous hydroelectric power plants.

Each of the seven participating states has an agency charged with the primary responsibility of protecting and advancing its rights and interest in the Colorado River system. As a group, these agencies constitute an interstate forum for addressing Colorado River problems and resolving interstate disputes.

The Secretary can make final decisions when the seven state agencies cannot agree or oppose an activity or judgment he considers essential. However, significant unilateral action on his part is unlikely, since it is subject to immediate legal and political challenge by the participating states. The development and operation of the Colorado River is therefore in practice a cooperative endeavor: multi-purpose, interstate, and geographically delineated by the watershed.

The Tennessee Valley Authority (TVA), as established in *Tennessee Valley* 1933 during the first term of President Franklin D. Roosevelt, *Authority* was also multi-purpose and interstate, covering a region coincident with the watershed of the Tennessee River (Figure 26a, page 52). The President proposed the Authority as

> a corporation clothed with the power of government but possessed of the flexibility and initiative of a private enterprise. It should be charged with the broadest duty of planning for the proper use, conservation and development of the natural resources of the Tennessee River drainage basin and its adjoining territory for the general social and economic welfare of the nation. This Authority should also be clothed with the necessary power to carry these plans into effect. . . .
>
> Many hard lessons have taught us the human waste that results from lack of planning. Here and there a few wise cities and counties have looked ahead and planned. But our nation has "just grown." It is time to extend planning to a wider field, in this instance comprehending in one great project many states directly concerned with the basin of one of our greatest rivers. (Roosevelt, 1933)

For years the Tennessee Valley Authority was visited by professional people from around the world as a model of regional river basin development, but it has not been copied elsewhere in the United States. Later, as shown in Figure 26a on page 52, the original TVA region was expanded for political reasons beyond the natural watershed of the river.

Since the Tennessee is a tributary of the mighty Mississippi, commercial navigation and flood control downstream were more important considerations than for the Colorado, and urban and agricultural water supply less vital in Appalachia than in the desert areas of the southwest. As an authority established by an Act of Congress, the three members of the TVA Board of Directors—appointed by the President of the United States and affirmed by the Senate—control and direct the functions the Authority has been delegated within the multistate region. By contrast, in the Colorado River Basin the Secretary of the Interior and seven designated state agencies function together by professional cooperation, negotiation, compromise, and political resolution in carrying out the legal responsibilities and limitations accumulated during 65 years.

The Mahaveli development project in Sri Lanka and the Delta project in The Netherlands, discussed on pages 156 and 157, are also examples of multi-purpose regional water projects undertaken and administered by national governments.

Transportation   In 1921 with the consent of Congress, the states of New York and New Jersey created the port authority, the first of its kind in the Western Hemisphere.

Port Authority   [Such an] authority is most effective where the program
of New York   to be carried out cuts across established political and geo-
and New Jersey   graphical boundaries; where the decisions to be made are primarily of a commercial or business character and the program is to be self-supporting, or the revenue principally based on user charges; where continuity of policy, planning, financing, and operation is crucial to the success of the program; and where the undertaking is neither attractive to private industry nor so deficit-ridden as to be impossible for self-support. (The Port of New York Authority, 1970)

The authority manages the major transportation facilities linking over 17 million people living in the New York metropolitan region with its economic and commercial heart centered on Manhattan island. The major airports, tunnels, bridges, containerports, and marine terminals that it controls constitute a transportation subsystem economically vital to a surrounding territory of some 4,000 square miles. Through these focal points flowed more than 300 million passengers in 1982. In recent years two different facilities have been added: the World Trade Center in lower Manhattan containing 9.5 million square feet of office space, and an industrial park in the south Bronx.

As its name indicates, the Port Authority of New York and New Jersey is a joint enterprise of two states covering an area of 1,500 square miles shown in Figure 57 on page 165. It is a civil governmental agency which cannot levy taxes, assess private property, or borrow on the credit of any state or municipality. To raise capital it borrows from banks or issues bonds secured by its revenues. In 1985 almost $6.5 billion were invested

Figure 57
**TRANSPORTATION: PORT AUTHORITY OF NEW YORK
AND NEW JERSEY**
Interstate
Public Administration
Operational
Reference: Port Authority of New York and New Jersey, *Comprehensive Annual Financial Report, for the Year End December 31, 1985*, New York (Port Authority of New York and New Jersey), 1986, 61 pp. *The ABC's . . . of the Port Authority of New York and New Jersey*, New York (The Port Authority . . . .), 1 October 1982, 20 pp.

in its two dozen facilities. Large additional investments expanding the three major airports serving the New York metropolitan area are planned during the next few years.

The authority is governed by a board of twelve commissioners, divided equally between the two states. However, their decisions are subject to veto by the governors of either the state of New York or New Jersey. As a civil governmental body operating financially much like a private enterprise, the Port Authority represents a regional planning activity unique in the United States.

land use   In 1978 Hawaii was the first state to officially adopt a com-
Hawaii prehensive state plan. It consists of state programs and functional plans, and county general plans. Years earlier in 1961 a land use law was enacted calling for the classification of all lands in the state and authorizing the adoption of rules, regulations, and procedures for determining land use throughout the islands.

The law now provides for four land use designations: urban, rural, agricultural, and conservation. Figure 58 on page 167 shows the disposition of these districts or zones on the island of Kauai, as originally determined by the state land use commission established for this purpose. Undoubtedly, they have been altered to some degree in the intervening years.

Urban districts are generally defined as lands in urban use with sufficient reserve to accommodate growth. Agricultural districts include lands with a high capacity for intensive cultivation, with a minimum lot size of one acre. Conservation districts are comprised primarily of lands in the existing forest and water reserve zones. Rural districts . . . are defined as lands composed primarily of small farms mixed with low density residential lots with a minimum lot size of one-half acre. (Eckbo, 1970)

The administration of these land use controls is complex: involving counties, the dominant city of Honolulu, and state agencies concerned with planning, economic development, natural resources, and taxation. The public at large—particularly private, business, and political interests—are also involved,

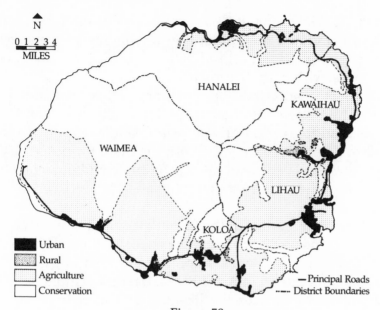

Figure 58
LAND USE: KAUAI, HAWAII
Intrastate
Civil Government
State Planning
Reference: "State of Hawaii Land Use Districts & Regulations Review,"
Eckbo, Dean, Austin & Williams, June 1970.

since the effects of land use restrictions on personal activities and prospects are widely recognized.

District boundaries can be changed by the land use commission through a process of petition and public hearing. Tax assessments are intended to encourage the prescribed uses of land and keep up to date with the changes in zone which will occur. Every five years, the commission is required by law to review the existing classification, districting, changes, and regulations relating to land use.

This system of land use control is equivalent to statewide zoning, subject to the same variety of actors and pressures that have characterized zoning since its inception in the United States in modern form in the early twentieth century. Because they cover large areas, most of the land use districts in Hawaii could as well be called regions. In all other states, except for Rhode Island, the four zones would be regional in size rather than district or local in their dimensions.

Florida   The Local Government Comprehensive Planning Act of 1975
(LGCPA) mandated that all local governments in the state of
Florida prepare, adopt, and implement comprehensive plans
for the area within their jurisdiction which incorporate land
use, circulation, conservation, housing, and coastal zone protection. These elements had to be internally consistent and
upon plan adoption, no private or public development could
take place except in conformity with the plan. Proposed development not consistent with the plan either could not take place
or the comprehensive plan must be amended as specified by
the LGCPA.

Serious inadequacies in the formulation and effectuation of
these local plans brought about revised legislation in 1985, enti-
tled the Local Government Comprehensive Planning and Land
Development Regulation Act (LPDA). It requires higher quality
local plans and increases the likelihood of their implementation. To assist this upgrading the state legislature voted funds
to be allocated among local governments specifically for this
purpose. If county and municipal plans do not meet the mandated content and quality, a district planning body is directed
to produce the plan and bill the local government for the cost
of its preparation. In addition, the governor and his cabinet
are authorized to impose financial sanctions on local governments whose comprehensive plans do not conform with legislated requirements.

The law also limits the amendment of local plans to twice
a year, except in emergencies and when called for by regional
developments. It states specifically that comprehensive plans
take precedence over any inconsistent land development regulation. A local government must adopt implementing land
developments within one year after submitting a revised plan.
The state Department of Community Affairs (DCA) is authorized to take action in court if the local government fails to adopt
the required regulations. An "affected person" can challenge
the DCA's determination that the local plan conforms to the
state law. A "substantially affected person" can initiate administrative review to determine whether land development regulations are consistent with the local plan. An "aggrieved and
adversely affected person" can challenge whether specific
development orders are in agreement with the plan.

To achieve these purposes, Florida has divided the state into 11 districts, each consisting of between three and nine counties, as shown in Figure 59 on page 169. The boundaries of the districts coincide with the outer borders of the counties they contain. The districts are roughly the same size. They do not intentionally coincide with particular physical or socioeconomic regions on the ground.

They are created to provide another level of consideration intermediate between state and local planning, between the

Figure 59
LAND USE AND PHYSICAL FACILITIES: FLORIDA
Intrastate
Urban and Regional Planning
Operations
Reference: Office of the Governor, Tallahassee, Florida, 3 March 1986.

smaller size counties and municipalities and the much larger area of the state as a whole. It is believed that adding regional planning will reduce poor performance by requiring higher quality local plans and promoting their implementation. Establishing districts for this purpose is similar to the organizational subdivision of continental France into 21 regions shown in Figure 62 on page 183.

A regional planning council is mandated for each district. It must prepare and adopt a comprehensive regional policy plan which includes a description of the natural, economic, and social characteristics of the district or region, performance standards for physical development, and implementation strategies. The purposes of the plan are specified:

1 Implement the goals and policies of the state comprehensive plan.
2 Assist the state in determining whether state, district, and local plans are consistent.
3 Guide the implementation of federal, state, district, and local government programs.
4 Provide a regional basis for the coordination of governmental activities, problems, and issues that are larger than local in scope.
5 Identify significant regional resources.
6 Guide the development of the district.
7 Develop public policy to resolve district issues.
8 Develop criteria for environmental impact evaluation.
9 Ensure that all actions by government officials within the region are consistent with the adopted plan.

Realization of Florida's mandated system of land use planning is a large order indeed. With the addition of district regions, there are four levels of government: state, district, county, and municipal—not to mention the special districts which perform a single function, produce a product, or perform a service. It is a complex system that symbolizes the fundamental difficulty of achieving effective regional planning when the number of different levels and units of government involved cannot be reduced by consolidation or elimination, and when each level resists relinquishing any of its decision making to another governmental body regardless of inefficiencies or unrealized opportunities.

Regional planning involves relating the areal jurisdictions of local governments to spatial conditions on the ground. Often this cannot be done unless the areas of a number of adjoining governments are coordinated or combined to encompass the regional situation in space. This requires an appropriate division, assignment, or integration of certain powers which until now have been the prerogative of each separate government.

> The Growth Management Act of 1985 . . . is supposed to guarantee that population doesn't grow faster than the physical means to support it. . . . Schools, roads, sewers, parks, libraries and assorted other infrastructure should be in place, or at least under contract, before developers throw up new houses and condominimums.
>
> In the next three years, every one of Florida's local governments—459 counties, cities, and towns—must draft a master plan, or update an existing one, describing how it intends to cope with future growth. . . .
>
> Each document must lay out a "level of service" for transportation, health care, education and so on, that fits with the existing population. Once accepted by the state, the community can't issue building permits, or approve zoning changes, that would cause a deficit in those service levels.
>
> Since the plans have the force of law, communities must follow the blueprint or risk penalties, such as the loss of state aid on infrastructure projects. (Carlson, 1987)

The Florida system represents the ultimate in physical land use planning by legislative mandate. It takes the time and attention of many people. More money than is now allocated is required to prepare better plans and ensure their implementation. The increased effort to fulfill legislated plans and procedures may produce excellent results. But there are now four levels of government together with special districts and a multitude of individual and organizational participants with different loyalties and interests. And there are the inevitable difficulties of achieving constructive cooperation. If for these reasons and because of its complexity the mandated planning process produces operational gridlock, it must be modified if it is not to be treated by lip service or benign neglect.

Truly comprehensive planning, which includes the operational activities of all government departments and agencies as well as physical land use planning, will be even more difficult to achieve by a process completely ordained from above.

coastal zone management   Coasts have always been important geographically, politically, and economically. Frequently they are governmental boundaries and potential lines of defense. They are the end points of surface transportation on land and on water where goods and people are transshipped. They are often where air passengers transfer between planes and aircraft are refueled. They are locations of dynamic physical forces and unique environments.

> Breaking ocean waves can deliver more than ten times as much energy to intertidal communities as solar radiation delivers. The result is a biological productivity that far outstrips that of the most fruitful rain forests. (Lewin, 1987)

Waterfronts are the necessary or preferred location for the terminals, processing plants, storage, U.S. Customs offices, and other installations required by industrial, commercial, civil governmental, and military activities that relate to ports, harbors, and other facilities along the coast. Scenic features of the oceanfront attract residential concentrations to the point that "walls" of closely spaced houses and apartments along the shoreline can make public access to the beach difficult or impossible in populated places. Coastal areas are the locus for water sports and recreation, and the unique habitat of certain animals, biological organisms, and botanical species.

For these reasons special attention is paid to land uses and activities along coastlines. In the United States, the Coastal Zone Management Act of 1972 authorizes federal grants-in-aid to states

> to encourage them to develop comprehensive management strategies for dealing with coastal resources. Working with affected local governments, the states prepare management programs for future uses of coastal lands and

waters, based on existing state and local government authorities, to be augmented when necessary by new state legislation. The programs emphasize protection of especially valuable coastal areas and facilitate appropriate development . . .

Programs approved by the Department of Commerce are eligible for continued support at 80 percent.

A vital intergovernmental feature of the Act is the "federal consistency" provision. This provision requires federal agencies to conduct their coastal activities consistent with federally approved state management programs. . . .

In 1976 Congress added a Coastal Energy Impact program [which] provided grants and loans to coastal states to help them to cope with the environmental and infrastructure impacts of energy activity in coastal areas . . . particularly with onshore impacts resulting from offshore petroleum activity. . . . (Office of Coastal Zone Management, 1979)

As would be expected in a federated republic, coastal situations and programs vary widely among the 50 states. Coastlines range from 13 miles in New Hampshire to 6,640 miles in Alaska including its Arctic coast. The average is approximately 250 miles. Thirty-two states have no ocean coastline.

Coastal zones established under the federal act are typically longer and narrower than other regions. Most of them contain areas that are very different one from another: geographically, geologically, economically, politically, socially, and in other ways. Their common feature is their location along the coast. In states with established programs, state or local coastal commissions preempt or influence land use control by counties and municipalities.

A federal presence is also established by the coastal barrier resources system created by Act of Congress in 1982. It discourages development in ecologically sensitive shorelines, bays, marshlands, and wetlands by withholding federal expenditures, grants, and damage insurance in coastal areas subject to hurricanes, severe erosion, and other destructive hazards.

The system now extends along 666 miles of the Atlantic Ocean and Gulf of Mexico shoreline covering 450,000 acres.

The U.S. Department of the Interior has proposed increasing these to 1,157 miles and 1,464,000 acres, excluding the Pacific coast and the shores of the Great Lakes.

The California Desert Conservation Plan described on page 174 is another effort by the federal government to establish effective regional planning covering productive operations, recreational activities, and areas needing conservation in environmentally sensitive regions. Such efforts result from the growing conviction that the use of areas which are nationally significant as well as locally important should be carefully planned rather than randomly developed. This applies also to regions where excessive use of water, lack of conservation, or surface pollution are depleting irreplaceable water resources. Likewise, the disposal of nuclear waste, toxic chemicals, and infectious bacteriological materials requires regional rather than local solution.

Implicit in these efforts is stimulus or intervention by the federal government as one of its responsibilities in the national interest. Important questions are raised. Should the federal government be directly involved with other environmentally sensitive or nationally important regions, such as high-altitude Alpine areas, the Arctic tundra, or prime agricultural land? Will such involvement require national land use policies and planning programs in the future? Can this be accomplished in a federal republic of 50 states before the opportunity to prevent irreversible deterioration or to avoid a crisis has passed?

conservation   One-fourth of the state of California is a desert, a distinctive geographical region subject in recent years to increasing use for various recreational, residential, commercial, and industrial purposes.

Today, the physical manifestations of these human pressures have become evident across the entire desert landscape: over 1000 communities, ranging in type from one-person mining settlements to resorts; large industrial mining operations and thousands of speculative digs; canal-fed agricultural valleys; nine military bases and testing grounds; 11 electrical power generating plants; 3,500 miles of high-capacity power transmission lines; 12,000 miles of oil and gas pipelines; over 100 communication sites on ridges and mountain tops; 15,000 miles of paved and maintained road; and thousands more miles of roads and ways cut solely by motorized vehicles. (Bureau of Land Management, 1980)

To these installations have been added in recent years several thousand wind-driven electric power generators and many new resorts and vacation homes. These activities are occurring in a complex patchwork of lands controlled by governmental agencies, military services, public and private commercial and industrial organizations, Indian tribes, and several hundred thousand individual property owners. Much of the territory is a checkerboard of adjacent square-mile tracts in different ownerships created under old settlement laws.

Rapidly expanding uses of open desert land by motorized off-road recreational vehicles have damaged large areas of ecologically sensitive desert environment and destroyed important archaeological sites. This intrusion, coupled with increases in other present and potential uses of land in the desert, calls for regional planning rather than random development.

Unlike stimulating economic development in regions such as southwest France or Appalachia in the United States, discussed on subsequent pages, the need in the California desert is conservation: directing or controlling the strong forces that exist for accelerated development.

Accordingly, in 1976 the federal government enacted a law to direct the management of public lands in the United States. A special section of the Federal Land Policy and Management Act required the preparation of a comprehensive long-range plan for the California desert conservation area shown in Figure 60 on page 176.

The goal of the Plan is to provide for the use of the public lands and resources in the [region], including economic, educational, scientific and recreational uses, in a manner which enhances whenever possible—and which does not diminish, on balance—the environmental cultural, and aesthetic values of the Desert and its future productivity. (Bureau of Land Management, 1980)

Figure 60
CONSERVATION: CALIFORNIA DESERT
Intrastate, Intercounty
Civil Government, Geography, Environment
Operations
Reference: Bureau of Land Management, *The California Desert Conservation Area Plan*, Sacramento, CA (State Office), 1980, 173 pp., maps.

The plan covers the 12 million acres of public land administered by the Bureau, one-half of the total conservation area. Formulation of the plan was a complex analytical and politically difficult undertaking. It required several years and numerous public hearings because of the diverse environmental considerations involved and the sharply competitive and often contradictory demands on the desert by different interests.

The elements for which specific management plans were prepared include: cultural resources; native American reservations; wildlife; vegetation; wilderness; wild horses and burros; livestock; recreation; motorized vehicle access; geology, energy and minerals; energy production and utility corridors; and land tenure adjustment. Also covered in the plan are areas of critical environmental concern and special areas, the process required to implement and amend the plan, and support activities and budgetary requirements.

The California desert is a region defined by its primary geographical characteristics and ecological systems. Although the Serengeti shown in Figure 36 on page 74 is a very different geographical region than the California desert, plans for their preservation and development each contain a migratory element. Planning for the Serengeti is based in large part on the migration of more than a million wildebeest. A primary concern of the desert plan is the "migration" of 16 million human visitors and many thousands of off-road motorized vehicles into the area every year.

As noted above the Bureau of Land Management covers only about one-half of the total area. Its public properties are scattered throughout the desert area and interspersed with other ownerships. Air force and marine corps bases, two weapons centers, a military reservation and a gunner range, two large national monument areas, and a state park cover approximately one-quarter of the region. Several sizable municipalities and many small communities are present. Mineral extraction and other industrial and commercial enterprises are scattered throughout the desert.

All of these diverse ownerships, activities, and interests must be reconciled for the most effective planning of the region. This requires cooperation by federal, state, county, and municipal governments, industries and commercial enterprises, Indian tribes, and the thousands of individuals owning or controlling property.

The Kingdom of Saudi Arabia is a unique country in several *national* important respects. As its name indicates, it is a kingdom with *development* highly centralized control by the king, crown prince, and royal family of some eight thousand members. Only two percent of its land is arable without irrigation. One-fifth of the country is desert, labelled on maps as an "empty quarter." But the country contains the largest reserves of crude oil of any nation in the world.

During the years after the establishment of the Organization of Petroleum Exporting Countries (OPEC) in 1961, Saudi Arabia's gross national income was multipled by increases in the price of crude oil, its predominant export. This new-found wealth produced one of the highest per capita incomes in the world when the services provided free by the national government are taken into account. These include complete medical care and completely subsidized education, which is paid for in whole or in part by the recipient in most countries.

Greater national wealth presented an opportunity to build a host of new facilities and provide additional services, in effect to transform the country from an underdeveloped to an industrially developed nation. This called for extensive planning at several levels of civil government. It required importing almost 2.5 million workers and specialists to provide construction labor and the technical skills unavailable in Saudi Arabia at the time.

Planning of a particular kind was required for a country one-third the size of the United States, but with a total population of less than 10 million people, one-quarter of whom are foreign workers. With a low population density of about six persons per square mile, large concentrations of people in a few cities, and surrounding nations understandably envious of Saudi Arabia's wealth and enormous oil reserves, heavy expenditures were needed to develop military forces for national defense.

This concern with national security also resulted in the subsidization by the national government of a vast expansion in the agricultural production of wheat, intended to nullify any attempt by other nations to pressure Saudi Arabia by withholding food imports (Rosewiez, 1986). And several schemes, one highly imaginative requiring towing icebergs to the Saudi coast, have been considered to supplement internal water supplies.

In its nonmilitary national planning, Saudi Arabia makes a particular use of regions. The spatial divisions incorporated in the four successive five-year development plans are not bounded by some predominant physical feature of the land (Figure 61, page 179). They are an outgrowth of the unification of five emirates by King Abdul-Aziz (1876–1953). Later, King Faisal bin Abdul-Aziz (1904–1975) took another step in the unification begun by his grandfather by eliminating the historical names of the six sections of the country. Among his ten commandments was one officially designating five regions by their geographical location—central, north, south, east, and west—and the sixth desert area as the "empty quarter."

These five areas are nodal regions according to the definitions adopted in this book. Each contains a central or most influential city which is the political, economic, social, or spatial focus of the surrounding area. Most of the population in the region, its territorial leaders, and dominant institutions are located in this central place. They determine in large part the general situation and particular condition of the dependent regional area. Regional boundaries are indeterminate zones rather than precise lines, but they are shown in the development plans as linear borders.

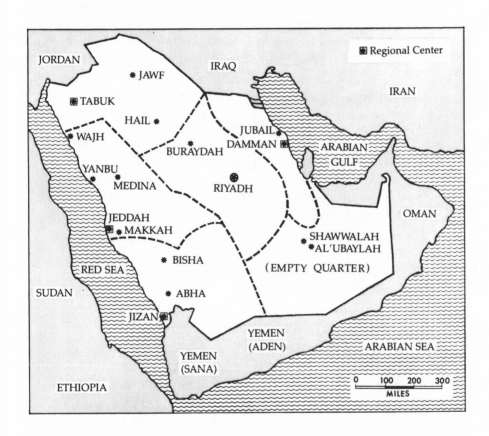

Figure 61
NATIONAL DEVELOPMENT: SAUDI ARABIA
National
Government
Operational
Reference: Ministry of Planning, *Fourth Development Plan*, 1405–1410 A.H. [1985–1990 A.D.], Kingdom of Saudi Arabia (Ministry of Planning Press), 24/2/1405 A.H., 24 February 1985, p. 1.

Although physical features do not demarcate the planning regions, Saudi Arabia does have distinct geographical differences between different parts of the country. In the heart of the kingdom is a vast, high, eroded plateau with the capital Riyadh at its center. Clockwise, the eastern area is the wealthiest part of the country containing the nation's oil resources, the administrative capital and port of Damman, Ras Tanura the world's largest petroleum port, and the new industrial complex of Jubail. To the southeast is the Rub al-khali (empty quarter), a quarter million square miles of desert composed of the largest continuous body of sand in the world. The western area of the country bordering on the Red Sea contains the Hejaz Asir mountain chain, Jeddah the major business center of the kingdom, and the religious centers of Mecca and Medina attracting over two million pilgrims every year.

National development trends during the first 5-year development plan focused on the establishment of the physical infrastructure for the main cities with high priority given to providing urban areas with water and sewerage systems, while regional development during the period of the [second and third national plans] was viewed in terms of expansion of infrastructure and municipal services to cover the rural areas . . .

The Kingdom is geographically divided into six regions. . . . While for planning purposes the Kingdom is divided into five regions . . . [and] administratively into fourteen Emirates (according to the administrative division of the Ministry of the Interior). . . .

The imbalance between regions is the focus of the regional problem in the Kingdom. The Ministry [of Planning], represented by the Regional Planning Department, is trying to reduce regional disparities through the attempt of allocating the financial and economic resources among Emirates according to their needs. . . .

Historically, regional imbalances resulted from the scattered nature of population settlements and from the concentration of natural endowments. Increasingly, interregional imbalances arising from the paucity of natural resources are being corrected by advances in technology, by the completion of infrastructure and by the rapid extension of public services to rural and remote areas. . . .

The completion of basic infrastructure and the industrial facilities . . . at Yanbu and Jubail, and the inauguration of downstream hydrocarbon industries, have further strengthened regional diversification outside the traditional urban centers. Industrial and agricultural loans and subsidies have spread opportunities outside the traditional centers for these activities, and the provision of services, including health, education and rural roads, has meant that the quality of life in rural areas has considerably improved. . . .

In general, the central and western regions (which include the largest urban centers) are considered the most diversified regions and also enjoy the highest level of service provision. While most regions enjoy a high level of service provision, it is worth noting that large disparities occur within the regions themselves. (Bajnaid, 1986)

The above report indicates generally the present method of allocating the portion of national income for civil government among the five planning regions, and the subsequent division and administration of these funds among the emirates which vary widely in the number and size of the municipalities they contain, and therefore in their relative importance.

As time passes and politics permit, it is intended that regional objectives and strategies will be closely integrated with the national development plan. In turn, the effectuation of regional plans will be more closely coordinated and administered by the emirates.

Local development needs will be identified more accurately by improved methods of collecting and maintaining local information. National developmental, regional, municipal, and rural planning will coalesce gradually into a well integrated progression of analysis, decision, programming, and effectuation. This will require a new class of competent middle managers.

Social and economic equality between and within the five planning regions will tend to increase as time passes and national developmental intentions are achieved. But productive and other activities will still vary among these regions according to the

location of resources, geographical and other natural conditions, and the specific objectives of civil planning.

National planning by Saudi Arabia exemplifies the use of
nodal regions and planning procedures designed to meet current political and socioeconomic realities, and to support more
highly integrated planning at the regional and municipal level
some time in the future.

organization   Historically, the French government has been highly centralized for almost 200 years. It is organized into 90 departments, and 36,700 communes—the smallest administrative unit
in France, governed by a council and mayor. In addition, each
ministry in Paris provides its technical services through its own
administrative area. The total number of administrative units
in France—a country four-fifths the size of the state of Texas—
is one-third more than the total number of local government
units in the entire United States.

In 1959–60, the government divided continental France into
21 districts or regions, each composed of from two to eight
departments (Figure 62, page 183). Usually, the Prefect of the
largest department in the region is designated Regional Prefect:
head of the decision making interdepartmental administrative
conference composed of the prefects of other departments in
the region and those responsible for technical services. This
conference disposes the funds allocated to the region by the
central government, which collects 90 percent of the taxes—
except for the Paris region where the percentage is less.

> The objectives of French regional planning . . . can be
> briefly summarized as the reduction of regional dispari-
> ties, with the control of the growth and excessive central-
> ization around Paris, the development of the underdevel-
> oped west and south, and the regeneration of problem
> industrial areas. . . .
>
> Inter-regional planning in France has the advantage of
> a well-tried, accepted, and effective framework of national
> planning . . . setting down guidelines for economic growth
> [achieved] by the use of the range of economic tools at [the
> government's] disposal. . . . Since 1947, [seven] major plans
> have been produced and implemented.

[A] system of [industrial location] incentives and controls has been complemented by a policy of increasing public investment in infrastructure in the problem regions. . . .

The growth center approach has . . . been developed   *policy*
as an integral element in French plans for decentralization and regional development, and . . . a policy of building up counter magnets in the form of *metropolis d'équilibre* throughout France to counterbalance the influence of the Paris region and provide foci for regional development was officially endorsed. . . . [Figure 63, page 184]

Intra-regional planning in France tends to be synonymous with the attempt to deal with the metropolitan scale problems of the Paris region. . . . (Glasson, 1978)

Figure 62
ORGANIZATION: FRANCE
National
Public Administration
Operational
Reference: Underhill, Jack A., with Paul Brace and James Rubenstein,
French National Urban Policies and the Paris Region, New Towns, Washington,
DC (U.S. Department of Housing and Urban Development, HUD-513-
IA), April 1980, p. 39.

Boundary of
Southwest Development Region

● Counterbalancing Capitals   ◉ Towns Assimilated to Counterbalancing Capitals
▥▥ Planning Zones for Counterbalancing Metro Centers   ◉ New Towns
▭▭ Planning Zones for Supporting Towns in Paris Basin   ◉ Supporting Towns in Paris Basin

Figure 63
POLICY: FRANCE
National
Public Administration
Operational
Reference: Underhill, Jack A., with Paul Brace and James Rubenstein,
French National Urban Policies and the Paris Region, New Towns, Washington,
DC (U.S. Department of Housing and Urban Development,
HUD-513-IA), April 1980, p. 17.

Regional planning does not originate in the regions, directly responsive to local needs and priorities; it is a mechanism for effectuating the national plan on a regional basis.

The Prefect of Paris, the chief executive of the Paris region, is appointed by and reports to the Prime Minister of France. Unlike provincial regional prefects who are assigned this additional duty by the department in which they are employed, the Prefect of Paris or Délégué General is a full-time position. Members of his staff are civil servants, drawn for the most part from one of the traditional ministries, assigned to the Paris region for varying lengths of time. He is the chief executive of the Council of Administration for the region, which advises the national government on physical planning and capital investment in the Paris area.

The director of the regional planning agency of the Paris region reports to the prefect.

> [The Agency] has many functions: creation of the general planning documents and policies with which jurisdictions in the region must comply; undertaking regional studies and regional forecasts; research and innovation; communication and publications; and serving as planning consultant to regional and local administrations and aiding development corporations in France and abroad. Three-quarters of the funding for the agency comes from a special tax on development in the region and one-quarter from contracts both in France and abroad. (Underhill, 1980)

Present planning policy seeks to control the growth of Paris. In addition to taxes and credit measures, pricing and fiscal provisions are compelling firms and households to pay more of the social cost of locating or remaining in the city. Enterprises already located in Paris are prevented or discouraged from expanding the physical space they now occupy. Further growth is encouraged in the five new towns built within the Paris region at some distance from the city, or at one of the growth centers being developed in other parts of the country.

Specific goals or plans for the Paris region include creation of new urban centers in the suburbs, directing growth along the axes upon which the five new towns are located, and preserving open spaces in the region. By creating urban centers balanced between the inner and outer suburbs, it is expected that commuting and transportation problems will be reduced, public services and facilities will be improved, and greater choice in employment, housing, and leisure time activities will be provided.

Regional planning has been a public policy for a longer time and a more advanced national activity in France than in any other country of the free world. In large part this has been possible because of her history, the competence and traditional dedication to public service of the professional bureaucrat, and the limited participation of the ordinary French citizen in governmental affairs outside the voting booth, political pressure, and protests in the streets of Paris.

development

southwest France

Unlike the Appalachian program described on page 189 requiring cooperation among 13 states, the development of France's southwest region—one of the largest underdeveloped areas in western Europe—is conducted by the French national government (Figure 64, page 187). To a greater extent than in the United States the central government in Paris determines and directs the economy of the country in general and its primary instruments of production specifically. Since the seventeenth century it has been concerned with the location of industry; and since the end of the Second World War it has undertaken the diversification of what was primarily an agricultuural economy. Spearheaded by its regional development agency (The Délégation pour l'Aménagement du Territoire), a 10-year plan for the economic development of the southwest region was launched by French President Giscard d'Estaing in 1979, one of the most ambitious regional development efforts since Italy began to industrialize the impoverished southern sections of the country in the 1960s.

The timing and scope of the plan for the southwest region was as much a political as an economic decision. The French government favored membership of Spain and Portugal in the European Common Market (ECM) to consolidate democracy in these neighboring lands. On the other hand, farmers and small industrialists in the southwest region feared that membership of these two nations in the ECM would result in cheap imports which could threaten their livelihood. The French government

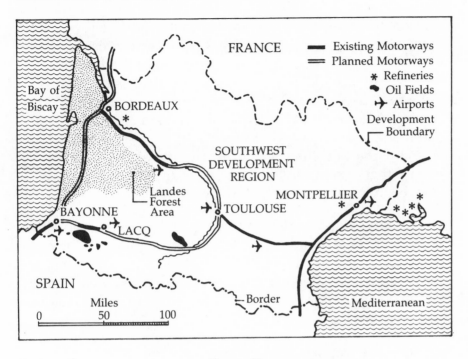

Figure 64
DEVELOPMENT: SOUTHWEST FRANCE
Intranational
Economics, Public Administration
Operational
Reference: Lewis, Paul, "The Eyes of France Are on 'A Kind of Texas,' "
The New York Times, 19 October 1980, p. 6E.

believed this opposition would be dissipated by the economic benefits produced by the regional development project in the late 1980s.

During the plan's first five years, the government . . . promised to allocate $1.2 billion largely to improve roads, docks, and airports. . . . The French government wants to attract modern, high-technology industries to the southwest that can benefit from the proximity of such big university towns as Toulouse, Montpellier and Bordeaux. . . .

Secondly, the planners want to encourage more efficient exploitation of the area's natural resources, particularly the great forests of the Landes, south of Bordeaux.

The natural gas fields at Lacq will start to decline [by 1990].
But meanwhile the Government is backing an exploration
drive as well as a solar energy program in the Pyrenees.

Finally, the planners foresee a radical transformation of
the region's farms. Owners of poor-quality vineyards are
being paid to plow them up and switch to crops in greater
demand. . . .

But the big green gleam in the planners' eyes is the
hope that southwest France will become Europe's biggest
soybean growing area. . . . (Lewis, 1980)

This large regional development program covers more than
one-quarter of the land area of France. It incorporates the major
elements required in an endeavor of this size: physical
improvements, economic incentives and investment, natural
resource exploration and exploitation, and experimental productive projects.

The most important elements of the Tennessee valley project were flood control, navigation, and the generation of
hydroelectric power. To these was added in the Colorado River
development project water supply to southern California and
Arizona. For the Delta project in The Netherlands the primary
purpose was land reclamation from the sea. For the Mahaveli
project in Sri Lanka the facilities required to irrigate a large
regional area were the main objective. Besides the intended
contribution of these new public works to the regional economy, they provided recreational areas and stimulated the establishment of new productive enterprises.

Development planning proposes whatever projects or activities are needed to improve the economy and social conditions
of a depressed region. Large engineering installations may or
may not be included depending on circumstances and the purposes of the development effort. Normally, economic development policies and programs promote new and expanded
industries, commercial enterprises, and transportation facilities. Health, education, and communication systems may need
to be changed or supplemented. Political problems are almost
certainly involved and must be resolved in the formulation of
the plan and program of effectuation.

This was the political situation and these were the regional *Appalachia* objectives when the federal government undertook to improve the depressed economic state and poor social conditions existing in parts of 13 adjacent states located along the Appalachian mountain chain in the eastern United States (Figure 65, page 190). Appalachia was established as an economic development region by an act of Congress in 1965. The region covers 190,000 square miles in 397 counties. Over $5.2 billion of federal aid has been spent by the Appalachian Regional Commission since 1965, an average of about $600 thousand per year per county.

The commission consists of the governors of the 13 Appalachian states (or their alternates), with a permanent federal co-chairman appointed by the President with the advice and consent of the Senate. The state members elect annually one of their governor members as the states' rotating co-chairman. Project proposals must originate in the states and be presented to the commission. No project can be approved unless it is first approved by the state concerned, and all recommendations of the commission must be approved by a majority of the governors and the federal co-chairman.

After 23 years of sporadic support by the federal government, limited collective action by the 13 states, and partial success, the Appalachian Regional Commission is being discontinued.

> In most respects, Appalachia is too diverse politically, physically, economicaly, socially, and in resources to be treated as a planning entity. With the exception of [specific] regional plans to be discussed, regional planning in the Appalachian context is to be understood as the development of general regional goals, regional strategies, and regional policy instruments but with state or area specific goals, priorities and institutional adaptations to accomplish them. Thus there cannot exist a regional plan in the sense of a single comprehensive document that defines goals, programs, projects and other activities for each individual area. (Newman, 1972)

This cooperative form of planning and development, requiring at least occasional modifications of self-interest in favor of the

Figure 65
DEVELOPMENT: APPALACHIA
Intranational, Interstate
Economics, Public Administration
Operational
Reference: Appalachian Regional Commission, *1980 Annual Report*,
Washington, DC (Appalachian Regional Commission), 31 March 1981,
p. iv.

collective benefit, is in sharp contrast with the unqualified authority of the three-person board of directors of the Tennessee Valley Authority and the control of the French government in Paris over regional development. It is probably the main reason why the socioeconomic development of Appalachia has been only partially successful. In addition, the active interest, persistent concern, and funds appropriated by the federal government have not been enough to achieve the professed purpose.

The percentage of the population of the Appalachian Region living below the federal government's poverty income level has been reduced from 33 percent in 1960 to 14 percent in 1980. Infant mortality has dropped by some 60 percent during the 1960s, and about 1.1 million more people moved into the region during the 1970s than migrated elsewhere. The economic base of the region is no longer almost exclusively coal and agriculture. But the region still lags behind the nation in employment and education, and there are pockets of severe poverty deep in the mountains.

People continue to migrate from the countryside to cities. *metropolitan* Almost 75 percent of the population of the United States lives *government* in cities, and it is expected that one-half of the world's population will be urban within the next several decades. A substantial proportion of the urban growth has occurred in metropolitan areas where central cities and surrounding legally independent municipalities—once spatially separate—have coalesced into one continuous built-up area extending for many miles (Figure 44, page 102).

There are many inefficiencies and frequent contradictions in separate planning by the many contiguous municipalities and other governmental units found in metropolitan regions. One way of greatly improving this situation is to establish a single governmental authority for the central city and surrounding area. It plans and administers those operating elements that are vital to the functioning of the entire metropolitan region. To this end, it is reported that some 16 cities and counties in the United States have merged since the Second World War.

An example of this form of consolidation in West Germany is the city of Hannover and its surrounding area. A greater Hannover area or metropolitan region has been created consisting of two parts: the central city of Hannover, and an outer surrounding ring of land which would be called a metropolitan area or county in the United States (Figure 66, page 192).

In 1986 population of the nodal city (535,000) almost exactly matched that of the surrounding area (543,000). But the area of the city was less than one-tenth of the 2,290 square kilo-

Figure 66
METROPOLITAN GOVERNMENT: HANNOVER, WEST GERMANY
Intranational
Civil Government
Operations
Reference: Zweckverband Grossraum Hannover, *Der Grossraum Hannover,*
Entwicklung Funktion, Hannover, West Germany (Zweckverband
Grossraum Hannover), 1982, p. 24.

meters (884 square miles) in the county. Most of the area in the metropolitan region was open space: more than two-thirds of the city, and over 90 percent of the county. The density of the city of Hannover was 9.8 persons per gross acre, 33.8 persons per built-up acre. Comparable figures for the surrounding area were 0.96 persons per gross acre and 10.6 per built-up acre.

The governing body of the region is a metropolitan congress or commission of 28 members: one-half delegated by the city council of Hannover, the other half by the government of the county. Members of the metropolitan congress do not have to also be members of the city council or the government of the county; in practice, only about one-half of the 28 members serve on two governmental bodies. As a consequence, the congress is organized by political party rather than by city and county. Matters for action by the congress are prepared by an executive committee consisting of nine of its members, plus the directors or managers of the city, county, and metropolitan regional governments ex-officio. Subcommittees have been established for regional planning, transportation, economic growth, recreation, and other activities.

In 1982, the administrative staff of the region consisted of 101 persons, supported by personnel in the city and county governments for detailed planning, implementation, and operational management. Unlike many of the other metropolitan regions in West Germany, the Hannover metropolitan region not only prepares regional plans but is responsible for carrying them out.

Part of the regional budget of DM 216 million in 1982 (about $86 million) was derived from an assessment of DM 92 million on the city and county. About one-half of the budget is spent on transportation. Substantial investments were made in new industrial, commercial, and regionally significant recreational areas. The region has been able to establish new areas occupied by commerce and industry despite the everpresent concern of businesses with the taxes they pay at these locations.

As would be expected there have been metropolitan regional conflicts as well as agreements. Between 1974 and 1980 there were disagreements between the region and the city and county concerning waste disposal. Similar disagreements are being thrashed out at the present time between local governments in the United States. So far, the city of Hannover and the county agree with the disposition of land uses within the metropolitan region made by its congress in accordance with the transfer of this power from local to regional government in 1981. Over-densification of the central city of Hannover has been avoided by a program of growth centers dispersed throughout the region, begun in 1967.

regional   General principles and practices of urban and regional plan-
planning ning can often be applied beneficially in different places at different times. But every geographical, socioeconomic, and political situation is unique, at least in its details calling for particular
treatment.

As indicated in Figure 67 Long Island is a particular region in important geographical respects. It is an island 116 miles long, never wider than 16 miles. Its western end is only a long stone's throw from Manhattan. Further west and to the north across Long Island Sound lies the most populous and extensive metropolitan region in the United States. The southern half of Long Island's 12,000 miles of shoreline, bordering on the Atlantic Ocean, is known for its fine beaches and its tidelands.

Density of population and building drops progressively from the boroughs of Brooklyn and Queens in New York City eastward to Nassau county, and again in Suffolk county which occupies approximately one-half of the island's 1,400 square miles of area. Woodlands, croplands, pastures, and marshlands are interspersed with urban places supporting industrial, commercial, recreational, educational, and other activities of almost every kind.

> Long Island is America in microcosm. We have [more than] 2.5 million people—that's a greater population than half the states. We're agricultural, industrial, coastal . . . urban as well as suburban and rural. . . . (Koppelman, 1974)

> If order can be imposed on the chaotic pattern of growth of the last 25 years, if an increasing population can be induced to settle where the island can comfortably absorb it, rather than where developers happen to own property;

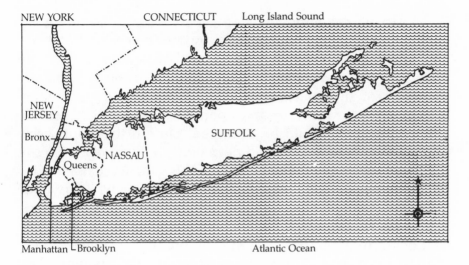

Figure 67
**REGIONAL PLANNING: NASSAU-SUFFOLK COUNTIES,
LONG ISLAND**
Intrastate
Civil Government
Operational
Reference: "Long Island At the Crossroads," *Newsday*, Special Reprint,
1978, p. 48.

if the island's remaining open space and natural resources
can be preserved and its blight erased . . . regional planning will have come of age. . . . (Jacobs, 1974)

In 1965 the Long Island Regional Planning Board was created by the Nassau and Suffolk county governments to address
the mounting problems of haphazard urban growth, traffic
congestion, and environmental deterioration occurring within
their jurisdictions covering two-thirds of the island outside New
York City.

The result, after five years of survey and study, was the
Nassau-Suffolk Comprehensive Development Plan. It proposed preservation of as much open space as possible by land
use designation, project design, or government purchase. In
keeping with this basic objective growth would be directed
according to a concept called the three C's: corridors, centers,
and clusters. The land uses prescribed in the plan conformed
to these spatial objectives.

Industrial development would be concentrated along the east-west central corridor formed by the Long Island railroad and automobile expressways physically linking Long Island with New York city and the rest of the nation. Commercial and residential growth would be directed around existing centers of activity with low density and open land uses in between. To this end houses would be clustered without the front, back, and side yards found around detached single-family homes in the usual subdivision. The portion of this yard space not needed in the cluster design forms a surrounding "greenbelt" of open space belonging to the homeowners association or other collective organization.

Soon after its publication the comprehensive development plan was formally approved by both county governments. This does not prevent modification or exception to the plan by either party, but it has remained the directive force for 15 years—so much so that in 1986 Suffolk county allocated $60 million to purchase permanent open space, a rare action by a local government in the United States.

During these 15 years the staff of the regional planning board conducted the studies required to keep the comprehensive development plan up-to-date and to improve it with respect to the events, changes, and proposals that occur continually in such a dynamic part of the greater New York metropolitan region. The staff also provides the specific analyses needed in connection with the steady stream of requests for the board's approval of land uses and proposed projects. Background studies were completed on population growth, commercial development, industrial location, employment, and the journey to work. In addition, the subjects of additional studies sponsored by the board indicate the broadening scope of its inquiry and action: groundwater preservation, coastal conditions, waste treatment management, dredging and spoil disposal, oil spill, and hurricane damage. These achievements were made possible by prior events and continuing support.

On June 28, 1960, Governor Rockefeller offered a 60-year development policy for the state [of New York] that considered regionwide planning for Long Island an essential first step. And the U.S. Department of Housing and

Urban Development was insisting on regional approaches before releasing planning study funds. More than $1,000,000 in federal cash has been the lifeblood of the Nassau-Suffolk agency since 1965 [now the Long Island Regional Planning Board]. (Morris, 1970)

In 1969 Washington designated the Nassau-Suffolk Planning Board as the official reviewing agency for all requests for federal assistance for public works programs in the two counties. Five years later, the Nassau-Suffolk region was designated a standard metropolitan statistical area by the U.S. Bureau of the Census, providing the region with a socioeconomic, political, and statistical identity distinct from its mammoth neighbor next door.

These supportive actions were not spontaneously generated in Washington. They were promoted by a few individuals in Long Island concerned about the consequences of inadequate or poor planning. For over 20 years, several local legislators—and the professional planner who initiated, energized, and directed the effort from its beginning—worked long and hard to establish bi-county regional planning as an influential and permanent part of local government, supported by government officials and the voting public. As with so many new endeavors, a single or several individuals are mainly responsible for their realization.

As is true for any comprehensive planning with significant objectives, not everything proposed in the Long Island Comprehensive Development Plan has been achieved. Many of the transportation improvements recommended, some of them involving other governmental agencies, have not been constructed. As might be expected in a region with higher than average incomes, few moderate and low income housing units have been built.

An important part of civil planning is the role and composition of its governing body. This determines if it is politically feasible to form such a body in the first place and whether it will function successfully once established. As noted in Chapter 3, metropolitan regional planning is rarely achieved in the United States. If each of the many municipalities and several counties comprising a large metropolitan region wants to be represented directly on the governing body, this produces a very large organization unable to direct the complex management of a metropolitan region. Insistence on membership signifies that regional planning is not considered important enough to arrange the primary prerequisites for its success: establishment of a representative governing body small enough to function effectively and to direct comprehensive regional planning; and division of operating activities among participating local governmental units according to their capacity to perform.

There are substantial differences in the governance of regional planning activities described in previous pages. The Southern California Metropolitan Water District illustrates the complications of inclusive representation in the management of a single public service: one of such immportance, however, that it is said that the history of California is in large part the history of water development. As noted previously (page 155), there are 135 members of the water district representing the cities served, 51 members on its board of directors, and between 16 and 18 members on each of seven standing committees. The Colorado River Compact is carried out cooperatively by the river commissions of seven states (page 163). The board of directors of the Tennesee Valley Authority, on the other hand, consists of only three members appointed by the President of the United States subject to approval by the Senate (page 164). And the Port Authority of New York and New Jersey is governed by a board of twelve commissioners divided equally between the two states, their decisions subject to veto by the governor of either state.

The Long Island Regional Planning Board has ten voting members. Six are lay people, three from Nassau county and three from Suffolk county. They are nominated by the county executive—the chief administrative officer of the county—ratified by the county legislature. The county controller and the county commissioner of public works are voting members of the board ex-officio. They contribute operating knowledge and experience concerning budgetary realities and physical facilities.

This composition of the voting membership provides a constructive combination. The six lay members represent the general public, and the county executive and legislature also if their nomination and confirmation of lay members establishes a continuing relationship. Four professional members represent the technical, practical, and operating aspects of regional planning. Lay members retain the majority vote on the board.

Representation is further extended by the addition of six officials, three from each county government ex-officio and without a vote: the county executive, presiding officer of the legislature, and planning director of the board.*

The total membership of 16 people represents the public interest and the managerial, budgetary, political, legislative, and professional planning concerns of the two constituent counties. All of the most important elements in metropolitan regional planning are included. Maintaining this broad representation when there are more than two counties in the metropolitan region would result in an oversized board.

The planning board formulates policy and provides the overall direction for joint regional planning by Nassau and Suffolk counties. The two county planning commissions carry out planning programs designated by the board, administer zoning and subdivision regulations, evaluate environmental impacts, conduct needed studies, and perform other activities relating to land use and physical facilities effectuating adopted plans. The board has the power, granted by the counties, to review their zoning regulations and variances; decisions by the board can be overridden only by an "extraordinary vote" of the town or village planning board concerned.

The exceptional record that has been achieved in Long Island is the product of professional capabilities essential for success in comprehensive urban and regional planning. Political acumen reduces the resistances to change and controversial issues characteristic of most legislators, or relates their support to their own self-interest. Forcefulness that does not arouse antagonism produces the momentum to effect improvements. Professional competence ensures the accuracy required for sound decision making and establishes the reputation for reliability that underlies public awareness and confidence. Without strong

---

*At the present time, the deputy director of the Suffolk County Planning Commission is the designated ex-officio member of the Long Island Regional Planning Board, because the present planning director of the commission is also executive director of the planning board.

motivation, time, and effort, the work required for comprehensive planning would never be complete or finished in time to meet deadlines.

In certain respects Long Island is more than an American microcosm. Because of its spatial constriction as an island and its proximity to New York city, it is subject to exceptional pressures for unrestricted growth to provide more housing within commuting distance. Long Island's recreational and vacation attractions could be overwhelmed by easy access. To control and plan further growth in an orderly fashion while maintaining the objectives of the comprehensive development plan is a challenge indeed.

The activities of the Suffolk and Nassau county planning commissions and the Long Island Regional Planning Board exemplify what can be accomplished by the present methods of urban and regional planning.

REFERENCES

[1] Atlantic Richfield Company, *1985 Supplement to the Annual Report*, Los Angeles, CA, 1985, pp. 26–35. [2] Bajnaid, M. Safwat, *Internship Report*, Regional Planning Department, Ministry of Planning, Kingdom of Saudi Arabia, Riyadh, Personal Communication, 16 September 1986. [3] Bratton, Lt. General, J. K., USA, Commanding, U.S. Army Corps of Engineers, "Emergency Operations," EP 500–1-3, July 1982, p. 1. [4] Bureau of Land Management, *The California Desert Conservation Area Plan*, Sacramento, CA (State Office), 1980, pp. 4, 5. [5] Carlson, Eugene, "Floridians Ponder Implications of State's New Planning Law," *The Wall Street Journal*, 20 October 1987, p. 43. [6] Department of Transportation, United States Coast Guard, Organization *Manual* (COMDTINST M5400.7B), Washington, DC, 1986, p. 1.1.1. [7] Eckbo, Dean, Austin & Williams, "State of Hawaii Land Use Districts & Regulations Review," June 1970. [8] Frankfurter, Felix, and James Landis, "The Compact Clause of the Constitution—a Study in Interstate Adjustment," *Yale Law Journal*, xxxiv, 1925, p. 702. [9] Glasson, John, *An Introduction to Regional Planning, Concepts, Theory, and Practice*, Second Edition, London (Hutchinson), 1978, pp. 368, 369. [10] Hundley, Norris, Jr., *Water and the West*, The Colorado River Compact and the Politics of Water in the American West, Berkeley, CA (University of California Press), 1975, p. xi. [11] Jacobs, David, "A long view of Long Island, The impact of planning on a city of suburbs," *The New York Times*, 17 February 1974, Magazine Section, p. 28. [12] Kaderali, Shiraz R., Director of Special Projects, Planning and Research, Pacific Gas & Electric Company, San Francisco, CA, Personal Communication, March 1987. [13] Kohl, Larry, "The Oosterschelde Barrier,

Man Against the Sea," *National Geographic*, October 1986, p. 527. [14] Koppelman, Lee, in: Jacobs, Lee, *supra*. [15] Landsman, S. H. (Compiler and Editor), *Annual Report for the Fiscal Year, July 1, 1984 to June 30, 1985*, Los Angeles, CA (The Metropolitan Water District of Southern California), 1985, p. 92. [16] Lewin, Roger, "Life Thrives Under Breaking Ocean Waves," *Science*, 20 March 1987, p. 1466. [17] Lewis, Paul, "The Eyes of France Are on 'A Kind of Texas,' " *The New York Times*, 19 October 1980, p. 6E. [18] May, Clifford D., "U.S. Coastal Plan Seeks to Expand Protected Areas," *The New York Times*, 24 March 1987, pp. 1, 11. [19] The Metropolitan Water District of Southern California, *Report to the California Legislature in Response to AB322*, Los Angeles, CA (The Metropolitan Water District of Southern California), March 1984, pp. 3, 5. [20] Morris, Tom, "The Hand that Shapes the Future," *Newsday*, 13 July 1970, p. 2R. [21] (NERC) North American Electric Reliability Council, *Annual Report 1984*, Princeton, NJ, 1985, pp. 3, 4, 8. [22] Newman, Monroe, *The Political Economy of Appalachia, A Case Study in Regional Integration*, Lexington, MA (Lexington), 1972, p. 70. [23] *The New York Times*, 24 October 1986, p. Y7. [24] Office of Coastal Zone Management, National Oceanic and Atmospheric Administration, Public Law 92–583, *Report to the Congress on Coastal Zone Management*, Fiscal Year 1978, Washington, DC (U.S. Department of Commerce), January 1979, pp. 6, 7. [25] The Port of New York Authority, *The Story of the Port of New York Authority*, New York, NY (Port of New York Authority), 1970, p. 32. [26] Roosevelt, Franklin D., The White House, 10 April 1933 (Display: TVA Exhibit, National Building Museum, Washington, DC, May 1986). [27] Rosewiez, Barbara, "Saudi Arabia Battles a Glut, but It Isn't the One You Think," *The Wall Street Journal*, 4 February 1986, p. 1. [28] Underhill, Jack A., with Paul Brace and James Rubenstein, *French National Urban Policies and the Paris Region New Towns*, Washington, DC (Department of Housing and Urban Development, HUD-513-IA), April 1980, p. 27. [29] Walsh, John, "Return of the Locust: A Cloud Over Africa," *Science*, 3 October 1986, pp. 17, 19.

Extensive human activities are subdivided into distinct administrative units to facilitate or make possible effective management of the organism as a whole. Each of these organizational units is associated with an area or region representing its administrative jurisdiction. Designation of these functional and areal subdivisions is as diverse as the kinds and forms of human activity they represent. They may be demographic, geographic, regulatory, operational, political, or military in nature. They may relate to sales, manufacture, distribution, or some other functional activity. The range of organizational purposes and designations is vast.

Existing jurisdictions rooted in history, custom, or law affect whether and how comprehensive planning can be accomplished.

Melville C. Branch, *Comprehensive Planning, General Theory and Principles*, 1983.

INDEX

AB

Since 1966, Melville ___ has been Pro____
at the School of Urb___ ___ ___nal Plan___
Southern California in ___ ___ ___

For almost a decade, h___ ___ in civi___
ning as a Los Angeles City ___ ___ing C___
years he was Corporate Asso___ ___be___
and a Member of the Senior Sta___
motive, electronics, and aerospace m___
in his career he was on the staff of the ___
Planning Board in the Executive Offices ___
D. Roosevelt, and Director of the Bureau o___
Princeton University. Dr. Branch has been ___
faculty at the University of Chicago and the Un___
ifornia, Los Angeles. He has consulted for public
organizations in the United States and abroad.

His graduate education includes a Doctor of Philos___
Regional Planning from Harvard University, the first adva___
degree in planning awarded in the world. He received the 1___
National Distinguished Service award of the American Planning Association for "outstanding sustained academic contributions to the planning field through numerous published books
and articles."

At least three of these publications are considered original
contributions. *The Corporate Planning Process* (American Management Association, 1962) was the first book on comprehensive planning by business. *City Planning and Aerial Information*
(Harvard University Press, 1971) was an expanded statement
of an earlier book pioneering the use of remote sensing in city
planning. *Comprehensive Planning: General Theory and Principles*
(Palisades Publishers, 1983) is the first book in the literature of
planning discussing common characteristics of this important
directive process and general principles of analysis and operation that apply whether it is conducted by civil government,
business, or the military services. His *Planning Urban Environment* (Dowden, Hutchinson & Ross, 1974) is believed to be the
first book on city planning in English translated into Russian
and published in the Soviet Union (Stroyizdat, 1979)